D1238146

J. Vernon McGee On Prayer

Published in Nashville, Tennessee, by Thomas Nelson, Inc.

Library of Congress Cataloging-in-Publication Data

McGee, J. Vernon (John Vernon), 1904–1988.
    J. Vernon McGee on prayer / by J. Vernon McGee.
      p. cm.
    ISBN 0-7852-6438-8 (hardcover)
    1. Prayer—Christianity—Sermons. 2. Sermons, American—20th century. I. Title.
    BV213.M34 2002
    248.3'2—dc21

2002003168

Printed in the United States of America

02 03 04 05 06 PHX 6 5 4 3 2 1

J. VERNON McGEE

On Prayer

PRAYING AND LIVING
IN THE FATHER'S WILL

DR. J. VERNON McGEE

THOMAS NELSON PUBLISHERS®
Nashville

A Division of Thomas Nelson, Inc.
www.ThomasNelson.com

CONTENTS

INTRODUCTION

ACCORDING TO MY HUMBLE JUDGMENT, THE greatest need of the present-day church is prayer. Prayer should be the vital breath of the church, but right now it is gasping for air. One of the great Bible teachers of the past said that the church goes forward on its knees. Maybe one of the reasons the church is not going forward today is because it's not in a position to go forward—we are not on our knees in prayer.

We seek out panaceas to resolve the conflicts of the world and to heal our own personal and private wounds. Many are consulting the psychiatrist, the doctor, the minister, and anyone else who will listen. But we do not seem to recognize that the great need in our own personal lives is prayer. In fact, prayer is the greatest neglected resource that we have; it's a power that we simply are not using today.

The disciples went to our Lord and said, "Lord, teach us to pray" (Luke 11:1 NKJV). They did not ask Him *how* to pray—they weren't looking for lessons on technique or an outline for ritualistic prayer. They had obviously heard our Lord pray, and they wanted to learn how to pray on the same high level as He did. That is a request many of us today need to make: "Lord, teach us to pray."

—J. Vernon McGee

PART I

Sermons On Prayer

WHAT JESUS
SAID ABOUT PRAYER

FOLLOWING JESUS IN THE DAYS OF HIS FLESH, we are struck by the prominence He gave to prayer. He gave a great reservoir of truth in this field. He not only talked about it, but, as you read the Gospels carefully, you will find that He Himself spent a great deal of time during His very busy ministry of three years *in prayer*.

Prayer today is the most neglected area in the life of the believer and in the life of the church. It is the weakest member of the body of truth. In fact, prayer deficiency has weakened every vital organ in the life of the believer and in the church today. It was the late A. C. Gaebelein who asserted that being alone with God and communing with Him is the strength of the Christian's life. There is a steady erosion that has worn away this strong foundation in the lives of believers. Andrew Murray, a great man of prayer, said that prayer is an index of the spiritual life. Most of our trouble and our problems can be traced back to the poverty of our prayer life. The neglect of prayer has affected all areas of the Christian's personal life and the total life of the church.

In the Gospel of Luke, our Lord uses a few brush strokes to produce four parable portraits of prayer. They are simply snapshots that can be slipped into your wallet—which makes them very practical. Putting these snapshots together gives us a composite picture of prayer.

Our Lord concluded chapter 17 of the Gospel of Luke with a discourse on the last days and the fact that He would be coming again. He likened the last days to the days of Noah—that they would be difficult days that would not be conducive to faith. Then He talked to His disciples about a life of faith in days that are devoid of faith.

> **Then He spoke a parable to them, that men always ought to pray and not lose heart.** (Luke 18:1 NKJV)

We are living in days, as He indicated, when men's hearts are failing them for fear. That is the reason why prayer is so pertinent for this hour.

The King James Version reads, "He spake a parable unto them to this end," that is, for this *purpose*: that men should always pray and not lose heart. He opened two alternatives to anyone who is living in difficult days. You and I must choose to do one of the two. Men in difficult days will either lose heart or they will pray; either there will be days of fear or days of faith. During World War II, when the bombing on the city of London was so intense, a sign appeared in front of one of the churches in London that read: "If your knees knock together, kneel on them!" That is practically a restatement of what our Lord has said, "Men always ought to pray and not lose heart."

It is the same thought that Paul put a little differently: "Pray without ceasing" (1 Thessalonians 5:17 NKJV). This does not mean you are to go to an all-day or all-night prayer meeting. Prayer is more an *attitude* of life than an *action* of the lips. Remember that Paul said to the Romans, "The Spirit Himself makes intercession for us with groanings which cannot be uttered" (Romans 8:26 NKJV). That is, they cannot be put into our *words*. Many times we do not have the words to pray, but we are praying nonetheless. Someone has put it in poetic language:

> Prayer is the soul's sincere desire,
>   Uttered or unexpressed;
> The motion of a hidden fire
>   That trembles in the breast.
> Prayer is the burden of a sigh,
>   The falling of a tear;
> The upward glancing of an eye,
>   When none but God is near.[1]

It is the entire life behind the words spoken that makes prayer effective. There was a famous preacher years ago who had many very unusual expressions. One of them was this: "When a man prays for a corn crop, God expects him to say

'Amen' with a hoe." You can't just stay on your knees all the time and pray for a corn crop. That's pious nonsense. But to pray for the corn crop, then go to work, is the thing our Lord is talking about in days when men's hearts are failing them.

PARABLE OF THE UNJUST JUDGE

What we have in this first parable is a relevant paragraph on prayer for the present hour. It is my firm conviction that our Lord never used a fictitious story when giving a parable. When Jesus told this story about the unjust judge and the widow, it probably was well known to the hearers of that day. They knew exactly the situation He was talking about. The story began like this:

> *There was in a certain city a judge who did not fear God nor regard man. Now there was a widow in that city; and she came to him, saying, "Get justice for me from my adversary."* (Luke 18:2–3 NKJV)

We're told that this judge was a godless fellow. He was an unscrupulous, scheming, cold, and calculating politician. Everything he did had to minister to his own advancement and satisfy his own ambition. He did not fear God. God had no place in this man's thinking. And since he did not fear God, he had no regard for man. He had no respect for this widow who was being treated unjustly and forced out of her little home. So the widow went to this prominent judge for help. She asked his secretary if she might talk to the judge, but the secretary told her, "He's very busy. If you will just tell me the nature of your complaint . . ."

So the widow told her, "I'm just a poor widow. I live out here at the edge of town, and I'm about to lose my place. It is unfair and unjust, and I want to appeal to the judge."

The secretary went into the judge's office and said, "There is a widow out there who wants to see you."

"Well," he said, "I can get rid of her in three minutes. I'm a politician, I know how to handle her. Let her come in." So she came in, he listened to her for three minutes, and then he said, "I'm sorry, but that's out of my realm. I'd *love* to do something for you, but I am unable to do anything. Good day."

The next day when he came into the office, there was the widow. He hurried into his office, called his secretary in, and asked, "What's that widow doing back?"

"She says she wants to see you."

"You go back and tell her I am busy until lunchtime."

"I've already told her that. But she brought her lunch. She says she will stay here as long as necessary."

The widow stayed all that day and didn't get to see him. He thought he had gotten rid of her. But the next morning when he came in, there she was! She did that for several days, and finally he said, "I'll have to do something about this. I can't go on like this."

Notice that our Lord recorded what the judge said to himself:

But afterward he said within himself, "Though I do not
fear God nor regard man, yet because this widow trou-
bles me I will avenge her, lest by her continual coming
she weary me." (Luke 18:4–5 NKJV)

The word *weary* is a very poor translation. I only wish it
were translated literally. What he said was this: "I must see
her lest she give me a black eye!" I don't know if he meant
a literal black eye—we are not told that the widow had
threatened him—but the very fact that a widow is sitting in
the judge's office every day doesn't look good. You see, he
was thinking of himself. He had gotten into office by saying,
"I'm thinking of the poor people," but he wasn't—he was
thinking of himself. "And lest she give me a black eye, I'd
better hear her."

So he told his secretary to let the widow in. This time he
said to the widow, "I'll give you legal protection." He called
up his man in her area and told him to take care of the matter. I imagine the man out there, who was also a politician,
said, "But she has no vote! She has no influence!"

"I know it," the judge says.

"Then why are you doing it?"

"I have been coming into my office every day for a week, and
she's sat here every day! She is giving me a black eye. I've got
to help her."

Parables were stories given by our Lord to illustrate truths.
The word *parable* comes from two Greek words. *Para* means
"beside," and *ballo* is the verb meaning "to throw"—(we get

our word *ball* from it). A parable means something that is thrown beside something else to tell you something about it. For instance, a yardstick placed beside a table is a parable to the table—it tells you how high it is. A parable is a story our Lord told to illustrate divine truth. There are two ways He can do this: one is by comparison, but the other is by *contrast*.

This parable that our Lord gave on prayer is a very simple story, yet it has been greatly misunderstood. I have heard many Bible teachers say that this parable teaches the value of importunate prayer. Although I don't like to disagree with men who are greater than I, that isn't so. This is not a parable on the persistency of prayer—as though somehow God will hear if you hold on long enough. This is a parable by *contrast*, not by comparison.

Listen to what our Lord had to say about this parable:

> **Hear what the unjust judge said. And shall God not avenge His own elect who cry out day and night to Him, though He bears long with them?** (Luke 18:6–7 NKJV)

He is saying, "When you come to God in prayer, do you think that God is an *unjust judge*? When you come to Him in prayer, do you think He is a cheap politician? Do you think God is doing things just for political reasons?" My friend, if you think this, you are wrong. God is not an unjust judge.

Why are God's people today so discouraged in their prayer life? If this *unjust* judge would hear a poor widow because she kept coming continually, then why do you get discouraged going to God who is *not* an unjust judge but who actually *wants* to hear and answer prayer? Don't you know, my friend, He is not unjust? We act as if we have to hold on to Him or He will not hear us at all. We don't have to hang on to His coattail and beg and plead with Him. God *wants* to act in our behalf! If we would come into His presence with an attitude of knowing that He *wants* to hear, it would transform our prayer lives.

PARABLE OF THE PERSISTENT FRIEND

And He said to them, "Which of you shall have a friend, and go to him at midnight and say to him, 'Friend, lend me three loaves; for a friend of mine has come to me on his journey, and I have nothing to set before him'; and he will answer from within and say, 'Do not trouble me; the door is now shut, and my children are with me in bed; I cannot rise and give to you'? I say to you, though he will not rise and give to him because he is his friend, yet because of his persistence he will rise and give him as many as he needs." (Luke 11:5–8 NKJV)

Let's bring this parable up-to-date. Imagine it's midnight and you are standing on your neighbor's front step, ringing the doorbell. He calls out, "Who's there?"

"It's me—your neighbor next door."

"What do you want?"

"I'm in grave difficulty. Remember I told you my aunt

from Iowa and my uncle from Texas were coming out to visit? I didn't know they were going to arrive here at the same time, but they both drove in tonight! Now, I was going down to the market tomorrow to lay in a supply of food to feed these folk because my aunt from Iowa and my uncle from Texas are accustomed to *eating!* I really wanted to feed them well. But I don't have anything. Would you mind getting up and letting me have a loaf of bread and maybe a little butter? If you've got a little bacon or ham there, would you let me have it?"

"Look, I've already gone to bed! My children are in bed, and I don't want to disturb my household. So go on back and put your aunt from Iowa and your uncle from Texas to *bed,* and we'll feed them in the morning." Then your neighbor turns over in his bed and pulls the covers up over his head.

But you put your finger down on the doorbell, and you begin to kick at the door.

By that time the baby is crying. He says, "Look, *go home! Let us alone!*"

"But I've got to feed my aunt from Iowa and my uncle from Texas. I wouldn't *dare* go back over there without some food for those hungry folks who have just come in from a long drive!"

Finally your neighbor says to his wife, "Well, it sounds like our neighbor is going to kick the door down unless I do something." So he gets out of bed, half awake and half asleep, goes to the refrigerator, digs out what he's got, brings it to the door, and hands it to you.

Perhaps you are saying, "I've been knocking at the door of heaven, but there has been no answer. God has not come to the door." My friend, do you think that God is asleep when you pray? He is not. "Behold, He who keeps Israel shall neither slumber nor sleep" (Psalm 121:4 NKJV). Do you believe that He does not want to answer your prayers? God *does* want to answer your prayers and He will. That is what this parable is saying. It is another parable by contrast and not by comparison. You do not have to knock down the door of heaven in order to attract God's attention. God is not reluctant to hear and answer you. He told us in Isaiah 65:24, "Before they call, I will answer; and while they are still speaking, I will hear." He knows what is in your heart before you ever put it into words.

Perhaps you are saying, "But He said no." Well, then, that's His answer. Our problem is that we do not like to take no for an answer. God *always* hears and answers the prayers of His own, but when He says no it is because we are not praying for that which is best for us. You have been answered. The difficulty was that you asked for ice cream, and when He came to the door He gave you corn bread. It wasn't what you wanted, but corn bread was the best thing for you.

When you go to the door of heaven and knock—and He says to come and knock—you are not coming as a neighbor from next door. You are a child who has come to your Father. We come to God as a *child* comes to a father. My friend, He is hearing only the prayers of His children. Are you a child of God? You can attend church, you can be religious and not be His child. How do you become His child?

But as many as received Him, to them He gave the right to become children of God, to those who [do no more nor less than simply] *believe in His name.* (John 1:12 NKJV)

When you have received Him as your own personal Savior, then you become His child. And when you pray to Him you are knocking at your *Father's* door. That changes prayer. You are not going to a God who is reluctant. You are going to a Father who wants to answer and *will* answer. You do not have to storm the gate of heaven to get God to answer your prayer. God has not gone to bed. The door is wide open, and He says, "Knock, seek, and ask." Take everything to God in prayer, and He will give you His very best.

But I say this very carefully: when we come into His presence we need to realize it is the Father's will that must prevail. When we come we must recognize that God is holy, that we are sinners, and that the most important thing in our prayers is not that we get something but that God's will might prevail. If you are His child and you desire the Father's will, He graciously opens the door and gives you your request.

PARABLE OF FATHERHOOD

We come now to the picture of a son:

If a son asks for bread from any father among you, will he give him a stone? Or if he asks for a fish, will he give

him a serpent instead of a fish? Or if he asks for an egg,
will he offer him a scorpion? (Luke 11:11–12 NKJV)

Our Lord looked around at the crowd that day—there were
many fathers there—and He said, "You, you're a father. If
your boy came to you and asked for bread, would you give
him a stone?" Of course no father would do that! So where
did we get the idea that we are better than God? If earthly
fathers want to be good to their children, don't you know
that the One who put a parent's heart in us has Himself a
father's heart? When you go to Him, you can expect Him to
do the very *best* thing for you.

Before the Day of Pentecost, our Lord stated it this way:

If you then, being evil, know how to give good gifts to your
children, how much more will your heavenly Father give
the Holy Spirit to those who ask Him! (Luke 11:13 NKJV)

Our Lord is saying here that the highest gift that any person
can receive is the Holy Spirit. And in order for the Holy
Spirit to be able to come and indwell every believer, God
had to give His own Son to die for us. The Lord Jesus died,
not only for our sins, but He died because you and I have an
awful sin nature. Writing to the Corinthians—and they
were carnal folk—Paul said:

Or do you not know that your body is the temple of the
Holy Spirit who is in you, whom you have from God, and
you are not your own? (1 Corinthians 6:19 NKJV)

Everyone who trusts Christ—that is, becomes a child of God—is *indwelt* by the Spirit of God today. He dwells *within* us! This wonderful transaction began in believers on the Day of Pentecost.

God today has already done for you the best that He possibly can do. To the Romans Paul said again:

He who did not spare His own Son, but delivered Him up for us all, how shall He not with Him also freely give us all things? (Romans 8:32 NKJV)

He will give us *all* things that are needful in our Christian life. He didn't say He would give you everything you *wanted*, but everything that you *needed*. Listen, my friend, if God gave His Son to die for you—and now has given you the highest gift, the Holy Spirit, to indwell you—do you think He will withhold from you *any* good thing? No, sir! He has already done the best.

Dwight L. Moody, in his inimitable way, used to illustrate this verse something like this: "Suppose I went to Tiffany's in New York, and Mr. Tiffany called me to the back of the store, opened the safe where he kept his most valuable jewels, brought out the biggest diamond he had, laid it on the showcase, and said, 'It's yours!' I would say, 'It's mine? You mean I don't have to pay you for it?' And he would say, 'I'm giving it to you.'" Then Mr. Moody would close his illustration by asking, "Do you think if he gave me that diamond that I would hesitate to ask him for a little piece of brown wrapping paper to take it home in?"

Don't you know that if God has given His Son to die for you, and if He indwells you by the Holy Spirit, He will not withhold from you any good thing? Do you believe that? Not many Christians believe that. They say, "Well, He's sort of holding out on me." My friend, if you are His child, He will do for you the very best He can. And the best He can do is the *best!*

PARABLE OF THE PHARISEE AND THE TAX COLLECTOR

We now look at our final picture. Oh, what trenchant and biting satire our Lord uses here! But He didn't do it to hurt them; He did it to help them.

> *Also He spoke this parable to some who trusted in themselves that they were righteous, and despised others: "Two men went up to the temple to pray, one a Pharisee and the other a tax collector."* (Luke 18:9–10 NKJV)

You could not get any two as far apart as these two men were. The tax collector was at the bottom of the religious ladder; the Pharisee was at the top. Tax collectors were grouped right down there with the sinners; the Pharisees were considered to be the most acceptable ones to God.

This Pharisee went into the temple to pray and make his sacrifice. As he stood and prayed, his priest was yonder in the Holy Place putting incense on the altar. In other words, this old Pharisee had it made. But listen to how he prayed:

The Pharisee stood and prayed thus with himself, "God, I thank You that I am not like other men—extortioners, unjust, adulterers, or even as this tax collector." (Luke 18:11 NKJV)

Isn't that an awful way to begin a prayer? Yet that is the way many of us do it. You say, "I don't do *that*." Yes, you do! Oh, we don't say it exactly that way—we've learned to say it better than that. But we have our own way of putting it: "Lord, I thank You I can give You my time and my service." How often I hear that! What a compliment that is for the Lord! Friend, we don't get anywhere in prayer when we pray like that. God doesn't need our service.

The Pharisee said, "I thank You that I am not like other men," and then he began to enumerate what he *wasn't*. "I'm not an extortioner"—evidently there was somebody around who was an extortioner. "I am not unjust. I am not an adulterer." Then he spied that tax collector way outside the temple, and he said, "And, believe me, Lord, I'm not like that tax collector! I'm not like that sinner out there." Then he began to tell the Lord what he *did* do:

I fast twice a week; I give tithes of all that I possess. (Luke 18:12 NKJV)

My, isn't he a wonderful fellow? Wouldn't you love to have him in your church?

Our Lord said he "prayed thus *with himself*." In other

words, he was performing a Hamlet soliloquy. Hamlet went off talking to himself and saying, "To be, or not to be, that is the question."[2] (And Hamlet is "off," by the way—he is a mental case.) Well, this old Pharisee was in the temple talking to himself—he thought he was talking to God, but his prayer never got out of the rafters. All he did was give himself a pep talk. He patted himself on the back and went out proud as a peacock. But God never heard that prayer.

Then there was the tax collector. Oh, he was a rascal! He was a sinner; he was as low as they come. When he became a tax gatherer, he denied his nation. When he denied his nation, as a Jew, he denied his religion. He turned his back on God. He took a one-way street, never intending to come back to God. Why did he do it? It was lucrative. He said, "There's money down this way." He became rich as a tax collector, but it did not satisfy his heart. We know from the story of Zacchaeus in Luke 19 that a tax collector's heart was *empty*.

And the tax collector, standing afar off, would not so much as raise his eyes to heaven, but beat his breast, saying, "God, be merciful to me a sinner!" (Luke 18:13 NKJV)

This poor man, in his misery and desperation, knowing that he had no access to the mercy seat in the temple, cried out to God. "God, be merciful to me a sinner" does not adequately express it. Let me give it to you in the language that he used: "Oh, God, I'm a poor tax collector. I have no access to that mercy seat yonder in the temple. Oh, if You could only make a mercy seat for *me!* I want to come."

> *I tell you, this man went down to his house justified rather than the other; for everyone who exalts himself will be humbled, and he who humbles himself will be exalted.* (Luke 18:14 NKJV)

Our Lord said *that* man was heard. Do you know why he was heard? Because Jesus Christ right there and then was on His way to the cross to make a mercy seat for him. John wrote:

> *And He Himself is the propitiation for our sins, and not for ours only but also for the whole world.* (1 John 2:2 NKJV)

Propitiation means *mercy seat.* Christ is the mercy seat for our sins, and not for ours only, but for the sins of the *whole world.*

The tax collector's prayer has been answered. Actually, today you don't have to ask God to be merciful. He *is* merciful. Many people say, "We have to beg Him to be merciful." My friend, what else do you want Him to do? He already gave His Son to die for you. He says to the very worst sinner, "*You* can come. There is a mercy seat for you." I have to admit to you that I had to come to that mercy seat. And if you want to be God's child, you'll have to come to that mercy seat where He died on the cross for your sins and my sins.

The penalty has been paid. The holy God is able to hold His arms outstretched. You don't have to beg Him, you don't have to promise Him anything, because He knows your weakness. You do not have to join something. You do not even have to *be* somebody. You can be like a poor tax collector. You can come and trust Him, and He will save you. God is merciful.

Chapter 2

THE PROPER
POSTURE OF PRAYER

I HAVE OFTEN WONDERED WHY THE CHURCH IN the past has not been divided on the subject of the posture of prayer. This is an issue that could divide the church, as it seems just about everything else has. The mode of baptism has certainly divided the church. There are those who believe sprinkling is the correct mode, a few believe pouring (that means getting a pitcher of water and dousing the head) is the correct mode, and others believe immersion is the correct mode. Still others believe you should be immersed not just one time, but three times. Then some say you should go down headfirst, and others say backwards. There are even some today who believe that if it's not done by running water then you haven't really been baptized. As you can see, baptism has certainly divided the church.

That's why I say it's a wonder that the posture of prayer hasn't divided the church. I'm surprised we don't have a group today known as "standers." They believe in standing up when you pray. Then it's a wonder that we don't have a group of "kneelers" who believe you should kneel down when you pray. Then there ought to be a group of "sitters." They believe you should sit when you pray. Then there's another group that believes you ought to lie down—they're the "liars." That would really be a large group! I didn't realize anyone else had considered this issue before, but then I discovered this poem called "The Prayer of Cyrus Brown."

"The proper way for a man to pray," said Deacon Lemuel Keyes, "and the only proper attitude is down upon his knees."

"No, I should say the way to pray," said Reverend Doctor Wise, "is standing straight with outstretched arms and rapt and upturned eyes."

"Oh, no, no, no!" said Elder Sloe. "Such posture is too proud. A man should pray with eyes fast closed and head contritely bowed."

"It seems to me his hands should be austerely clasped in front with both thumbs pointing toward the ground," said Reverend Doctor Blunt.

"Last year I fell in Hodkin's well, head first," said Cyrus Brown. "With both my heels a-stickin' up, my head a pointin' down, the prayenist prayer I ever prayed was a-standin' on my head."[1]

Is the mode of prayer, the posture of prayer, essential? May I say, categorically and dogmatically, no! The posture of the body at the time of prayer has nothing to do with the effectiveness of the prayer. God hears and answers prayer regardless of the posture of the body. It was Victor Hugo who said that the soul is on its knees many times regardless of the position of the body. The answer and the power of prayer are not determined by the posture. It is not essential, but it is important. The mode does not affect God, but may I say that the posture has an effect upon the believer and upon others. For the posture reveals the attitude of the life and of the soul.

Although it is not essential to effective prayer, Scripture still suggests several postures. You will find that standing in prayer is a scriptural mode. In fact, I think that was the mode used more often in the Old Testament than any other. If we look at it chronologically, the New Testament opens with Zacharias standing at the altar of prayer (see Luke 1:5–25). That's when God chose to break in and resume His communication with man. But it's also interesting to note something our Lord said concerning standing in prayer:

> *And when you pray, you shall not be like the hypocrites.*
> *For they love to pray standing in the synagogues and on*
> *the corners of the streets, that they may be seen by men.*
> (Matthew 6:5 NKJV)

The Pharisees liked to be seen, and therefore they stood when praying. But our Lord said that they were hypocrites. And He didn't let it go at that. He gave a parable about two men praying. As I mentioned in the last chapter, one was a lowly tax collector and the other a prideful Pharisee. Our Lord began the parable, "The Pharisee stood and prayed thus with himself" (Luke 18:11 NKJV). So He at least implies that standing in prayer has the element of ministering to the pride of heart; it has the potential of leading to a proud spirit.

So, then, what is the correct posture in prayer? May I suggest to you that kneeling, according to the Word of God, is the proper posture of prayer. I want to give you four instances—two from the Old Testament and two from the New Testament—of men who knelt in prayer and the great lesson that is taught through their examples. First we'll look at Solomon as he knelt in prayer at the dedication of the temple. Then there is Daniel, who knelt in prayer toward Jerusalem despite the decree that no man was to make any petition to anyone other than the king. And then we'll turn to the prayer of our Lord Jesus Christ when He knelt in the Garden of Gethsemane. Finally, we'll see Paul and the Ephesian elders as they knelt together in prayer down upon the seashore. In the prayer of Solomon we see *creature humility*. In the prayer of Daniel we see *courage*. In the prayer of the Lord Jesus Christ we see *commitment*. And in the prayer of Paul and the Ephesian elders we see *communication*.

SOLOMON: CREATURE HUMILITY

First let's look at the prayer of Solomon. Solomon was the king, and men bowed to him. There was no man on topside of this earth to whom he bowed. Not a one. He built the temple, which it's estimated today cost more than $5 million to construct and furnish. And do you know there was not a plaque on it dedicated to Solomon? Thank God for that! Today we call it "Solomon's temple," but the only temple Solomon ever had was on the side of his head. It wasn't his temple—it was God's. And Solomon gathered the people together and dedicated the temple to God.

> *For Solomon had made a bronze platform five cubits long, five cubits wide, and three cubits high, and had set it in the midst of the court; and he stood on it, knelt down on his knees before all the assembly of Israel, and spread out his hands toward heaven.* (2 Chronicles 6:13 NKJV)

There he stood, on a brazen platform high above all the people. He never was so high as he was on the day of the dedication of the temple; he was elevated to the pinnacle. And yet we see him going down on his knees before the almighty God. Glory had filled that temple as it had filled the tabernacle, and Solomon got down on his knees before God.

You see, man is a small creature on this earth. Man is a midget in this universe. Did you know that scientists have been able to detect out yonder galactic systems that went out of business billions of years ago but that are still sending back a message? When you look at man in relation to this vast creation, remember what David said:

When I consider Your heavens, the work of Your fingers,
the moon and the stars, which You have ordained, what
is man that You are mindful of him? (Psalm 8:3–4 NKJV)

So what is the proper position of this little creature who someone said is just a "skin disease on the epidermis of a little planet"? His proper position is down on his knees before his Creator! Even Solomon, in all of his glory and with the multitudes bowing to him, knelt before his God! That's where we belong today.

DANIEL: COURAGE

Now let's move on and consider Daniel, a great man of prayer. Daniel, as a young man, served under Nebuchadnezzar. As an old man, he again found himself in the service of a king. King Darius was an enlightened ruler. He knew the value of a man like Daniel, and so he lifted him to a position in which he really controlled the kingdom and all outside affairs. Daniel would correspond today to the vice president and the secretary of state rolled into one office.

Because this man, a Jew, was brought to such a high level, his enemies were jealous of him. They hated him, and they sought to trap him. But the greatest compliment concerning Daniel came from his enemies:

So the governors and satraps sought to find some charge
against Daniel concerning the kingdom; but they could

*find no charge or fault, because he was faithful; nor was
there any error or fault found in him. Then these men
said, "We shall not find any charge against this Daniel
unless we find it against him concerning the law of his
God."* (Daniel 6:4–5 NKJV)

In other words, "We can't find anything wrong with this
man. He is faithful in his office to the king and to his God.
You won't find any discrepancies in his bookkeeping, he's at
the office on time every morning, he doesn't leave until
quitting time, and he's loyal." So this crowd came
together—and they were a clever crowd, you can be sure of
that—and said, "The only way we can hurt him is through
his religion. But the king likes him, so let's go way out on a
tangent and get King Darius to make a rule that the people
are not to worship anyone except the king." Now that, of
course, appealed to Darius as it would to any ruler who is
eaten up with egotism, as many of them are. Darius was flat-
tered by the idea of having everyone come to him and no
one else. So he fell for it, and he signed a decree that no one
was to make a petition to anyone or any god except him.

Notice Daniel's reaction to this new law:

*Now when Daniel knew that the writing was signed, he
went home. And in his upper room, with his windows open
toward Jerusalem, he knelt down on his knees three times
that day, and prayed and gave thanks before his God, as
was his custom since early days.* (Daniel 6:10 NKJV)

Now Daniel didn't do anything that was foolhardy; he didn't fling the window open and pray. The window was already open, because it was his custom to pray three times a day with the window open toward Jerusalem. Nor did he do something cowardly and close the window. This man didn't let the decree affect him one whit. The courage of Daniel is evidenced by the fact that he would kneel down before God at a time like that.

I hear some people say today that if you just take everything to God in prayer He'll get you out of all your trouble, put you on easy street, and take the thorns off all the roses and all the stones out of your pathway. I do not know about that, but I do know this: Daniel prayed himself right into a lions' den. Those petty politicians caught him kneeling in prayer to God, and so they threw him in the lions' den. Daniel may have prayed himself into it, but we ought to add that he prayed himself out of it also.

JESUS: COMMITMENT

Let's turn now to the New Testament and the record that Dr. Luke gave of our Lord Jesus Christ in the Garden of Gethsemane:

> **And He was withdrawn from them about a stone's throw, and He knelt down and prayed.** (Luke 22:41 NKJV)

In this prayer of our Lord we have commitment— commitment to God. For it is in these prayers uttered in the

Garden of Gethsemane that He said, "Not My will, but Yours, be done" (Luke 22:42 NKJV). That is real commitment to God.

May I say also that He did more than merely kneel down. Matthew tells us:

He went a little farther and fell on His face, and prayed. (Matthew 26:39 NKJV)

He not only knelt down, but He actually got down on His face before God! May I say to you, He set a pattern that was followed by the first martyr in the church. For it's said of Stephen, "Then he knelt down and cried out with a loud voice, 'Lord, do not charge them with this sin'" (Acts 7:60 NKJV). Kneeling—that's the position that this man Stephen took when he prayed. He was following the example of our Lord. It was an expression of his absolute commitment to God.

My friend, today, if there ever was a time when God's people needed to get down on their knees and make a commitment of their lives to God, this is the day. How many of us still try to make our own decisions? We attempt to run the show the way *we* want it run, and we have no interest in taking orders from up yonder. We need to go down on our knees before Him! Commitment: even the Lord Jesus Christ in the Garden of Gethsemane got down on His knees and said, "Not My will, but Yours, be done." That is commitment to God.

PAUL AND THE EPHESIAN ELDERS: COMMUNICATION

I come to our final illustration, that of Paul and the Ephesian elders. These men demonstrated communication with others.

Paul had founded the church in Ephesus, and it is my belief that this was the finest church of all. The Ephesian elders loved Paul, and he loved them. Acts 20 records a tender meeting between Paul and the elders of the church in Ephesus. Paul was carrying the offering from the gentile Christians to the suffering saints in Jerusalem. On the way, he stopped at Miletus and called for the elders of the church in Ephesus to come down. Paul knew that when he arrived in Jerusalem there would be trouble and that he likely would not see his Ephesian brothers again in this life. It's one of the most tender meetings that you'll ever see.

Paul gathered them together and said, "Let's have prayer." So down on the seashore, the elders and Paul knelt in prayer.

And when he had said these things, he knelt down and prayed with them all. (Acts 20:36 NKJV)

They were not trying to show off—it was not like the Pharisees of whom the Lord said, "Do not be like the Pharisees who love to be seen of men when they pray" (see Matthew 6:5). These men were not trying to be seen of men, but they sure did communicate something there that day. I have a notion that many of the sailors who were down at the shore getting ready to go on a voyage, with fear and trembling in their hearts and wondering what the voyage would hold, looked at those men praying and said to themselves, "I wonder if they really are praying to the living and true God?" I have a notion that many of the loved ones of the men leaving drew near wistfully to hear what Paul and the elders were praying about. And I imagine there were a great many that had come down to the beach for a holiday who paused their cavorting on the sand to look at these men kneeling in prayer.

There was a Christian man who observed several Christian couples at a resort. He told me, "Believe me, even when they ate their hamburgers they didn't return thanks. You couldn't tell even on the Lord's Day that they were believers." How many today are giving a testimony by their lives to those about them? Christians today are afraid to be marked as a peculiar people. But I must say that there's something about being a peculiar Christian that makes an impression on people. I don't mean to make a spectacle of yourself or to be an oddball. He said that we *are* a "peculiar people," not to *act* peculiar (1 Peter 2:9 KJV).

Your life can give a testimony in a very natural way. I once sat in a hotel lobby and observed in the adjoining room a businessman at a cocktail party who took his glass, turned it upside down, and said, "Make mine ginger ale." If you don't think that had a testimony, I wish you could have seen the goggle-eyes of those who were already half drunk. I wish you could have seen them look at him. Believe me, he had a testimony. Without being odd, what is your testimony today? May I make a suggestion? You can witness by a posture in prayer.

When I was just a boy in my teens, I went to a Christian conference in Tullahoma, Tennessee. I was the problem child in that conference, so they said. I am sure that the leaders of that conference had no idea the effect they had on this boy. I'd never before seen anybody kneel in prayer, but that night in our cabin the counselor got us around— and we were a bunch of rowdy boys—and we all knelt in prayer. That has impressed me to this day: posture in prayer.

Let's conclude by looking at someone who really got in a kneeling position—old Elijah. You might know he would outdo anybody else!

> *So Ahab went up to eat and drink. And Elijah went up to the top of Carmel; then he bowed down on the ground, and put his face between his knees.* (1 Kings 18:42 NKJV)

You ought to try that. I tried it—it's the most awkward position in which to pray. I guarantee you'll stay awake if you try this posture of prayer. It's so completely uncomfortable that there is little danger of growing drowsy or absentminded while you're praying.

Oh, my friend, today we need to pray! Regardless of the position of the body, our hearts and lives should be on their knees before Him. In fact, we should be like Elijah and go down on our faces before Him.

DANIEL—
A MAN OF PRAYER

WE'RE LIVING IN A DAY WHEN WE NEED PRAYER as we've never needed it before. So I think it would benefit us to turn to Daniel, the man of prayer, for some direction on how to pray effectively. We think of Daniel as being a great man of prophecy. Our Lord even labeled him "Daniel the prophet." And he was a great prophet, but back of being a man of prophecy he was a man of prayer.

Chapter 9 of the Book of Daniel is one of the great chapters of the Bible. It has a double theme of prayer and prophecy. If one were to choose the ten greatest chapters of the Bible on the subject of prayer, this chapter would be included. If the ten most important chapters on prophecy were chosen, this chapter would again be included. The first twenty-one verses give us the prayer of Daniel, and it is those verses that I'd like to look at in detail.

Now this prayer of Daniel calls to our attention two very

important matters. First there are the *circumstances* of Daniel's prayer. Then there are the *conditions* of his prayer.

CIRCUMSTANCES

Let us first examine the circumstances of the prayer of Daniel.

> **In the first year of Darius the son of Ahasuerus, of the lineage of the Medes, who was made king over the realm of the Chaldeans—in the first year of his reign I, Daniel, understood by the books the number of the years specified by the word of the LORD through Jeremiah the prophet, that He would accomplish seventy years in the desolations of Jerusalem.** (Daniel 9:1–2 NKJV)

Now this is a very interesting statement that's given to us here. The date is around 538 B.C. The decree of Cyrus returning these people to the land came in 536 B.C. So when the ninth chapter of Daniel opens, it is about two years before the end of the seventy-year captivity. Daniel was a student of prophecy as well as a prophet. We're told here that he had Jeremiah's prophecy before him, and he read in Jeremiah that they were to be in captivity seventy years. Let's look at the prophecies for ourselves. They're very clear.

> **And this whole land shall be a desolation and an astonishment, and these nations shall serve the king of Babylon seventy years.** (Jeremiah 25:11 NKJV)

For thus says the LORD: After seventy years are com-
pleted at Babylon, I will visit you and perform My good
word toward you, and cause you to return to this place.
(Jeremiah 29:10 NKJV)

Daniel read that God said certain things about the captivity. He could look at the calendar and see that they had
only two more years to go. So he went to God in prayer
about it.

There are two things that are obvious here. One is that
Daniel *believed* in prophecy, and he believed that it was to
be fulfilled literally. When Daniel read "seventy years," he
didn't interpret it as some spiritual, mystical number or
twist it and make it mean something altogether different.
To him it meant exactly what it said. He believed the Word
of God, and he believed it literally. So when God said,
"You're to be in captivity seventy years," seventy years
meant seventy years!

The second thing we should notice is that the determining factor that brought Daniel to this prayer was his study of
the Word of God. I say to you, my beloved, that this is a very
wonderful thing. It's a tremendous thing. It's a great thing.
Today the Word of God is being discounted, watered down,
twisted, and distorted. So it's quite interesting to find a man
like Daniel taking the Word of God at face value, believing
it, and seeing it fulfilled. You see, the Word reveals the will
of God. A study of God's Word, followed by prayer, is the
formula for determining God's will.

CONDITIONS

Now let us note the conditions of prayer as revealed in this prayer of Daniel. I don't want to discourage anyone, but real prayer is not just spiritual sit-up exercises. Real prayer requires laborious effort. It requires arduous work, eternal endurance, and plenty of pain. Real prayer is an exercise of the soul that develops spiritual muscles. It tones up the new man so he can endure hardness in this world in which we live. So let's look at the basic elements that go into the prescription of prayer.

Purposeful Planning

First of all, I see purposeful planning in this prayer of Daniel. These are days when prayer is a hit-and-miss proposition. It's a sort of extracurricular activity of the Christian. It's not a vital breath as it was for God's men of the past. I recall the story of a little boy who shot his BB gun. A man asked him, "Sonny boy, what did you hit?" The boy answered, "Nothing." So the man asked, "Well, what did you shoot at?" And the boy again said, "Nothing." May I say to you that a lot of praying is like the little boy with his new BB gun—it aims at nothing and it hits nothing. But when Daniel went to God, he had a plan.

Daniel knew what he wanted. Listen to him:

> **Then I set my face toward the Lord God to make request by prayer and supplications, with fasting, sackcloth, and ashes.** (Daniel 9:3 NKJV)

He went to God seeking by supplication and by prayer. May I say to you that Daniel's prayer was not a marathon of words. It was not a putting together of pretty, periphrastic phrases and counting them off like beads on a rosary. He didn't spout a lot of words but say nothing! He did not utter pious platitudes, prate about many things, or utter shopworn clichés.

After a meeting, a buddy once said to me, "Did you notice in there that So-and-So *read* his prayer?" I said, "Yes. What about it?" He said, "Do you think a person ought to read his prayer?" I said, "Well, when they read their prayer, they at least know what they're going to say beforehand. A lot of times you wonder what they've said even after they've finished. He at least knew what he was going to say."

This man Daniel knew what he wanted. His prayer was not vague or vapid or vacuous. He got right down to business with God. Oh, if we'd only learn to pray like that.

Powerful Petition

The second condition is powerful petition. I turn to the end of the prayer:

> *Now while I was speaking, praying, and confessing my sin and the sin of my people Israel, and presenting my supplication before the LORD my God for the holy mountain of my God, yes, while I was speaking in prayer, the man Gabriel, whom I had seen in the vision at the beginning, being caused to fly swiftly, reached me about the time of the evening offering. And he informed me, and*

talked with me, and said, "O Daniel, I have now come forth to give you skill to understand." (Daniel 9:20–22 NKJV)

Daniel went to God with a petition. I want to tell you that this man had a burden on his heart. He knew what he wanted, and he went to God about the matter.

Someone is sure to say, "Daniel read in Jeremiah that they were going to come out of captivity in seventy years, and he believed it. So why in the world did he pray about it? There's no need to pray for that which is already predestined." Have you ever heard anyone say that? "If a thing is predestined, there's no use praying about it. Prayer can't change things." Daniel didn't believe that. He believed you could change things. He believed that you were to pray about things that were already predestined. In fact, he believed those were the exact things you were to pray about!

You see, Daniel knew the will of God, and that gave him confidence when he went to Him in prayer. John said,

Now this is the confidence that we have in Him, that if we ask anything according to His will, He hears us. (1 John 5:14 NKJV)

Daniel had confidence that he was praying in the will of God, and that makes a petition powerful. (And believe me, my friends—he got his answer! The angel Gabriel appeared to give him his answer personally!) A great many of us do not have confidence when we go to God in prayer because we're not quite sure that the thing we are praying about is according to the will of God. How can you know the will of God? Well, you can't know it in a moment. You can't wait until the situation comes up and then immediately know the will of God. You need to be saturated with the *Word* of God. Beloved, you and I can never know the will of God apart from the Word of God. Why? Because the *will* of God is revealed in the *Word* of God. And this man, Daniel, had been studying the Word of God! So he went in and he petitioned God in confidence.

Daniel said, "Lord, You said this, and I'm here to hold You to it." You know, God likes to be held to His promises. I used to pray with a fellow back when I was in seminary. He tried hard to memorize Scripture, but he found the same difficulty many of us find: you can memorize it this morning, but you forget it by tomorrow. One morning he thought he had one memorized, a promise, and he got down on his knees and tried to quote that Scripture. I think he came at it a half a dozen times. He missed it every time. Finally, he got up, got his Bible, went back down on his knees, turned to the passage, and said, "Lord, here it is right here." You know, I think God smiled that morning. I think the Lord said, "Yes, that's it, and I said it." God likes it when we come to Him in confidence and hold Him to what He says in His Word.

The reason we pray all around a subject is because we're not sure of God's will. So we ask *everything*. We pray the kind of prayer that the Lord just can't miss. Our thought is that if we cover everything, maybe we'll get something through to Him. It's wonderful to know what you're after when you go to Him, to know it's His will, and then to lay hold of God in prayer for that matter. When we can lay hold of God in assurance and in confidence, then we have powerful petition.

Painful Performance

The third condition of prayer is painful performance. Let's look at this verse again:

> **Then I set my face toward the Lord God to make request by prayer and supplications, with fasting, sackcloth, and ashes.** (Daniel 9:3 NKJV)

Now somebody is sure to say, "McGee, I know exactly what you're going to say: that fasting and sackcloth and ashes were for the Old Testament, but under grace we're not subject to following this method." That's exactly what I'm going to say. You don't have to do this today. But I want to say something to you: this matter of fasting *is* for today. There are several Scriptures that back me up, although I'm not going to turn to them now. But Paul mentioned on several occasions that he prayed and fasted and he fasted and prayed. Someone may ask, "Does that do any good at all?" My friend, there is no merit in a flagellation of the flesh. But I will say one thing: it may not have any merit before God, but it'll do *us* a whole lot of good. It will reveal something of the sincerity and reality of our prayer life.

It is too easy today, friends, to pray. Paul wrote to the Romans:

> *Now I beg you, brethren, through the Lord Jesus Christ, and through the love of the Spirit, that you strive together with me in prayers to God for me.* (Romans 15:30 NKJV)

The word *strive* is not strong enough to express Paul's meaning. The word in the Greek is transliterated to come up with the English word *agony*. And in this verse there is put with it a preposition in the Greek that just intensifies it, and it means "great agony"! Paul said, "I want you to agonize with me in a great way!" Are we to agonize in prayer? Yes. It's too easy today. There are discipline and pain in prayer that are not in evidence today.

I'd like to share with you one of the prayers of Martin Luther. Remember that this is a prayer of the man who initiated the Reformation.

> O Almighty and Everlasting God! How terrible is this world! Behold, it openeth its mouth to swallow me up, and I have so little trust in Thee! . . . How weak is the flesh, and how powerful is Satan! If it is in the strength of this world only that I must put my trust, all is over! . . . My last hour is come, my condemnation has been pronounced! . . . O God! O God! . . . O God! do Thou help me against all the wisdom of the world! Do this; Thou shouldest do this . . .

Thou alone . . . for this is not my work, but Thine. I have nothing to do here, nothing to contend for with these great ones of the world! I should desire to see my days flow on peaceful and happy. But the cause is Thine . . . and it is a righteous and eternal cause. O Lord! help me! Faithful and unchangeable God! In no man do I place my trust. It would be in vain! All that is of man is uncertain; all that cometh of man fails . . . O God! my God, hearest Thou me not? . . . My God, art Thou dead? . . . No! Thou canst not die! Thou hidest Thyself only! Thou hast chosen me for this work. I know it well! . . . Act, then, O God . . . stand at my side, for the sake of Thy well-beloved Jesus Christ, who is my defence, my shield, and my strong tower.[1]

That's quite a prayer, isn't it? No pretty phrases there. Oh, but how it moved God and changed all of Europe. Now how about a modern prayer? One of our nice little up-to-date prayers? Listen to this one:

Almighty God, as I sit here this lovely Sunday morning surrounded by newspapers and half listening to one of the big preachers over the radio, it has just come over me that I've lied to Thee and to myself. I said that I did not feel well enough to go to church today. That was not true, dear Lord. I simply was not ambitious enough. I would have gone to my office had it been Monday morning. I would have played golf if it had been Wednesday afternoon. I would have attended my lodge meeting if it had been

Thursday evening. I would have gone to the picture show if it had been Friday night. But it's Sunday morning, Lord, and Sunday illness covers a multitude of sins. God, have mercy on me. I was not really ill; I'm lazy and spiritually cold and indifferent.

At least the prayer's honest, isn't it? But that's a modern prayer, if you please. Do you know why prayer meetings are not popular and there is so little praying being done today in the church? It's because real prayer is work. It's labor. It's pain! But we today are lazy and indifferent.

Perfect Plainness

Now we come to the fourth condition revealed here in the prayer of Daniel. After painful performance there is perfect plainness. Listen to Daniel:

We have sinned and committed iniquity, we have done wickedly and rebelled, even by departing from Your precepts and Your judgments. (Daniel 9:5 NKJV)

Then he went on and put a label on every one of the sins. He called a spade a spade. And when a sin was a sin, he labeled it that. We need to be candid, plain, open, straightforward, and without reserve when we go to God in prayer. Now you cannot speak plainly to some people—it's dangerous. They don't like it, and you get in trouble. And some people speak to us plainly, and we don't like hearing it either. But some folk just can't talk to you plainly, and we can't talk to them plainly. As a result, there's no real communication. But did you know that when you go to God you can be plain and candid? We need to go to Him like that more often. We may be able to put up a front with others, but we can't put up a front with Him.

God has been very plain with us. He said:

You lust and do not have. You murder and covet and cannot obtain. You fight and war. Yet you do not have because you do not ask. You ask and do not receive, because you ask amiss, that you may spend it on your pleasures. (James 4:2–3 NKJV)

How many times do we go to God and say, "Lord, do this for me so I can serve You better" when all the time we know down deep in our heart it's really because of some selfish reason? It's a manifestation of the flesh, and we're trying to cover it up as something good and holy. Don't you know, my beloved, that you can't cover that up before God? He says, "I didn't hear and answer your prayer when you asked with that pious reason, because I knew that down underneath you wanted to spend it on your own pleasures. I did not hear nor did I answer."

Paul called such a hypocrite "a double-minded man, unstable in all his ways" (James 1:8 NKJV). When we go to God, we pray for His will to be done in a certain manner, and all the time we're attempting to work it out our own way. We're double-minded. That's the reason why our prayer life is not vigorous and real. When we go to Him we can't be real, because we haven't been real down here. The psalmist said in Psalm 66:18 (NKJV), "If I regard iniquity in my heart, the Lord will not hear." Be candid with Him! Just go to Him and say, "Lord, I've been asking You for this, but if You really want to know the truth, I had a wicked motive in view. Oh, God, cleanse and purify my motives and my heart." He is frank with us, and we can be frank with Him.

But before you and I can have perfect communication with God, there must be confession of sin. He just won't let us go on with unconfessed sin. You may recall that Joshua, after the defeat at Ai, came before God and put on a good show by rolling around in the dirt. But in his heart he was pious, and he thought he could hide that from God. He said, "Oh, Lord, Israel has been defeated. And remember, Your name is at stake." Oh, how pious Joshua was! God said to him, "Joshua, get up off your face. Quit groveling in the dust like that and stop praying! Israel has sinned. You deal with that sin, and then I'll be prepared to hear your prayer." (See Joshua 7.) We need, my beloved, perfect plainness with Almighty God.

My friend, today you can go to God and you can unburden your heart. There's no use putting up a front before Him; He knows us already. Just tell Him how it is. He'll hear; He'll understand; and, if we're honest, He'll answer.

Personal and Private

May I mention something else: your prayer must be personal and private. I've often wondered why Daniel didn't hold a great big public prayer meeting over this matter. But he didn't. He went in personally before God and confessed for himself and for the nation.

Have you ever noticed that our Lord also prayed privately? There's no public prayer in the ministry of Christ. Yes, He prayed before groups, but they were personal groups—never public prayer. Public prayer should always be short; private prayer should always be long. That's where we need to spend time.

Plenary Penetration

The last condition for effective prayer is plenary penetration. *Plenary* means "full"—there must be full penetration. Did you know that the only thing that can penetrate outer space is prayer? Sir Isaac Newton, one of the earliest scientists, said that he could take his telescope and look millions and millions of miles into space. But then he could lay it aside, go into his room, shut the door, get down on his knees in earnest prayer, and see more of heaven and get closer to God than he could assisted by all the telescopes and material agencies on earth. That is plenary penetration.

What is it today that enables a little man to penetrate space and get to the throne of God? It's power. It takes power beyond man. That's the reason Scripture is careful to say that we are to be filled with the Holy Spirit. May I say that I do not believe God will hear, or *can* hear, prayer unless it is that of a Christian who is Spirit-filled. That's the reason why Jude, giving instructions for the last day, gave as the second instruction "praying in the Holy Spirit" (Jude 20 NKJV). And Paul, writing to the Ephesians, recommended "praying always with all prayer and supplication in the Spirit" (Ephesians 6:18 NKJV). There was an old agnostic of the past who said that prayer is a fool talking to himself. I'll admit, it is almost that *unless you're Spirit-filled*. You see, prayer must be supernatural to be real. What makes prayer supernatural is that the one doing the praying is filled by the Holy Spirit. Genuine prayer is the Holy Spirit speaking in the believer through the Son to the Father.

My beloved, there must be a divine enabling to pray effectively and efficiently. We need more power in prayer. After God crippled Jacob yonder at Peniel, He said to him, "You shall now have power with God" (see Genesis 32:28 KJV). Oh, how we need power with God today! And we get that power by being able to pray from the heart.

Chapter 4

PRAYER
AND POWER

FOR MANY TODAY, PRAYER IS THE WEAKEST LINK in their chain of Christian experience. Their prayers are not very meaningful, and there is a lack of satisfaction in their prayer lives. But may I say to you, our Lord never intended for it to be that way. He said:

> **And whatever you ask in My name, that I will do, that the Father may be glorified in the Son. If you ask anything in My name, I will do it.** (John 14:13–14 NKJV)

What potential and possibility are contained in those verses! You see, our Lord meant for prayer to be vital, real, and powerful.

In his epistle to the Ephesians, Paul presented the armor that the believer is to put on in order to meet the enemy, Satan. Every bit of that armory is for defense, with the exception of two weapons of offense, both of which are to be wielded in the power of the Holy Spirit. One of those is the sword of the Spirit, or the Word of God. But will you notice the second:

> *Praying always with all prayer and supplication in the Spirit, being watchful to this end with all perseverance and supplication for all the saints . . .* (Ephesians 6:18 NKJV)

Prayer, through the Holy Spirit, is a weapon of offense against Satan. You can't get much more powerful than that. Then Jude, who gave one of the most picturesque accounts of the apostasy that you'll find in Scripture, told the children of God:

> *But you, beloved, building yourselves up on your most holy faith, praying in the Holy Spirit . . .* (Jude 20 NKJV)

Praying in the Holy Spirit is what gives us the power to live the Christian life in these days of apostasy.

But did you know that it is impossible for us, being feeble and ignorant human beings, to live the Christian life all on our own? We are simply too weak and frail to measure up to God's standard, my beloved. Thankfully, God has not asked us to. He has, instead, provided us with a Helper, so that today the only way we can live the Christian life is by being filled with the Holy Spirit. Likewise, the potency of our prayer lives is in ratio only to how well we are being filled by the Holy Spirit. In fact, true prayer is possible only through the power of the Holy Spirit.

What does it mean to pray in the Holy Spirit? Let's turn to Paul for an answer:

Likewise the Spirit also helps in our weaknesses. For we do not know what we should pray for as we ought, but the Spirit Himself makes intercession for us with groanings which cannot be uttered. (Romans 8:26 NKJV)

The Holy Spirit makes intercession for us. Because of our ignorance, there are times when we honestly do not know what to pray for. That's the reason why we hear so many people reciting glib prayers as if they know exactly what God wants done. May I say, those prayers never get beyond the ceiling. When we are ignorant of the will of God and thereby what we should be praying for, that's when we need the Holy Spirit to lead us in our prayers. Have you ever gone to God about a matter and said from your heart, "Lord, I do not see the way clear, and I do not know what to pray for as I should"? May I say, if you are praying in the Holy Spirit there would come from your heart at that time a prayer: "Oh, God, not my will, but Yours, be done" (see Luke 22:42). You see, His will is the primary part of prayer. It is not primarily to get God to do something that *we* want done, but to get us to do something that *God* wants done!

Why is it that we do not know how to pray in the Holy Spirit as we ought? One of the reasons is because we do not have heaven's perspective. We do not see things as God sees them. John wrote:

Now this is the confidence that we have in Him, that
if we ask anything according to His will, He hears us.
(1 John 5:14 NKJV)

My friend, the condition for having our prayers heard and answered is that we must be praying according to the will of God. But there are many times we don't have heaven's perspective, and so we can't see His will clearly. I've heard preachers say, "God has given you a signed check—fill it out for any amount." Well, now, if you think God's handing out checks like that, you're wrong. God is a very good bookkeeper, and when He signs a check, He fills in the amount! We can't pray for just any old thing and expect Him to give us the answer we want.

Paul prayed for a thorn in the flesh to be removed. He had good reason to want that thorn removed: it was interfering with his work. I can well understand why Paul would say, "Lord, this thorn in the flesh is hindering me in my work for You, so please remove it." He took that prayer to God three times, and by the last time I imagine he had a tone of impatience: "Lord, You haven't heard or answered my prayer!" But God said, "Yes, Paul, I heard your prayer. Furthermore, I answered it. I'm not removing the thorn, but I'm going to give you grace to bear it." (See 2 Corinthians 12:7–9.) You see, He brought Paul into line with His will. Prayer is not for us to get God into line with our little will, but it's to get us into line with His will. Oh, how important it is to understand that today!

Because we do not have heaven's perspective, there are times when we pray for things that, should God answer the way we wanted Him to, would be the worst things in the world for us. I can look back over my life and name a dozen things for which I thank God He did not answer the way I thought He should have. There was one specific time when I prayed for Him to open a door. And I sure tried to help Him—I had a crowbar in that door, prizing it with all my might! I did everything to get through that door, but He slammed it in my face so hard that I can still hear the echo. I was disappointed at the time, but today I am eternally grateful to Him for hearing and answering my prayer according to *His* will instead of mine. That's the reason why we need to pray in the Holy Spirit.

Another reason why we struggle in our prayer lives is because when we pray without being filled with the Holy Spirit, we tend to be selfish and self-seeking. James, who was nicknamed "Old Camel-Knees" because he spent so much time on his knees in prayer, said:

> **You ask and do not receive, because you ask amiss, that you may spend it on your pleasures.** (James 4:3 NKJV)

I'd guess that if we were to make an inventory of our prayers, we'd find that nearly everything we pray for serves our own interest or affects us in some way. We pray for our own pleasures.

This is one of the worst things that can happen to a believer, and Scripture gives us abundant evidence of that.

When the children of Israel were out in the wilderness, they complained to God, "Oh, Lord, we're tired of manna three times a day. We want meat for dinner." So God said, "I'll hear and answer your prayer. I'll give you meat, and it'll stick in your teeth!" The psalmist wrote:

And He gave them their request, but sent leanness into their soul. (Psalm 106:15 NKJV)

Then there is the example of Hezekiah, who became sick unto death. God sent Isaiah the prophet to tell him, "Hezekiah, get ready—you're going to die." Hezekiah wouldn't even listen to Isaiah. He said, "I don't want to hear that bad news," and then he went to God in prayer, saying, "Oh, God, heal me! Don't let me die." God said, "All right. Isaiah, go back and tell Hezekiah that I'm going to give him fifteen more years." (See 2 Kings 20:1–6.) This may seem like an awful thing for me to say, but Hezekiah should have died when the time came for him to die. He could have gone down in God's book as an outstanding king. Instead, three things took place after God extended his life that showed him to be foolish: he showed his treasures to Babylon, which caused a great deal of trouble for Jerusalem later (see 2 Kings 20:12–13); he begat a son, Manasseh, who was the most wicked of any king (2 Kings 21:1 indicates that Manasseh was born after Hezekiah prayed for his life to be extended); and in his later years he revealed that his heart had become filled with pride (see 2 Chronicles 32:25). You see, it might have been better if Hezekiah had died at God's appointed time.

You and I need to be sure that what we are doing is according to the will of God. We can't do what we want to do and then ask God to bless it. God doesn't move that way. We have to go His route if we want to receive the blessing. We have no right to demand anything of God. It is true that He demands a great deal of us, but we are not to demand anything of Him. Elijah is given to us as an example of a great man of prayer. His greatest prayer was uttered with 450 prophets of Baal and all of Israel sitting in the gallery watching him. He stood before an altar dripping with water and asked for fire from heaven:

> *And it came to pass, at the time of the offering of the evening sacrifice, that Elijah the prophet came near and said, "LORD God of Abraham, Isaac, and Israel, let it be known this day that You are God in Israel and I am Your servant, and that I have done all these things at Your word. Hear me, O LORD, hear me, that this people may know that You are the LORD God, and that You have turned their hearts back to you again."* (1 Kings 18:36–37 NKJV)

Friend, I wish we would recognize the fact that if God doesn't do it, it's not going to be done. There is no room for selfish desire in prayer. We are to pray according to His will.

Have you ever noticed in the so-called Lord's Prayer that the first three requests concern God's glory and His will, and they do not concern us at all?

Our Father in heaven, hallowed be Your name. Your kingdom come. Your will be done on earth as it is in heaven. (Matthew 6:9–10 NKJV, emphasis mine)

In our prayers we need to be more concerned about seeing God's will done and not our own desires fulfilled.

Another problem is that we limit our praying to the physical and not to the spiritual. We pray for material things and not for the intangible. We evaluate things in relation to the realm in which we live. Have you ever noticed that our Lord values things very differently? You may recall the story of the widow who put a little mite not worth our one-cent penny into the offering. Then the rich people came in behind her and gave lavish gifts. Now, today we would commend the people who gave a lot. In fact, we'd probably name a fellowship hall after them! But may I say to you, our Lord watched it all, and He said, "Truly I say to you that this poor widow has put in more than all" (Luke 21:3 NKJV). May I say, He measures things quite differently from the way we do.

We can also turn back to a newspaper published two thousand years ago—the *Jerusalem Times*. On the front page, in great big boxcar letters, was the headline: "Caesar Signs New Tax Bill." Boy, that was real news throughout the Roman Empire. And if we thumbed through to the back page and looked under "Births," we would have seen this in little bitty type: "Born to Mary, baby boy named Jesus." Now I say to you that they got their headlines mixed up. You see, the birth of Jesus was headline material in heaven! We put the emphasis in the wrong place, emphasizing the physical and the material instead of the spiritual and miraculous as God does. Again, we know not what we should pray for, and therefore we are to rely on the Holy Spirit to help us pray in the will of God.

The Holy Spirit brings power to our prayers, my beloved. Notice what Paul said to the Ephesians:

> **Now to Him who is able to do exceedingly abundantly above all that we ask or think, according to the power that works in us . . .** (Ephesians 3:20 NKJV, emphasis mine)

For centuries, the tremendous power of the lowly atom lay dormant because no one knew anything about it or how to release it. Have you ever stopped to think that there may be other sources of power at our fingertips that we are absolutely ignorant of today? Well, I know of one: prayer. Prayer is a great, vast, and unexplored territory that we know practically nothing about. There is a reservoir of power there that has never been tapped.

Do you remember the story of Jacob wrestling with a man in the wilderness? I happen to believe that man was the preincarnate Christ. Jacob wrestled with Him all night long, refusing to yield. He put up his self-will until God said finally, "It's a last resort, Jacob, but I'll have to cripple you." And He did. We're told that the man touched the hollow of Jacob's thigh as he wrestled with him and put it out of joint. Then will you notice what happened next:

And He said, "Let Me go, for the day breaks." But he said, "I will not let You go unless You bless me!" (Genesis 32:26 NKJV)

Jacob was forced to stop wrestling and instead he just held on. He found out that you do not get anywhere with God by struggling and resisting. The only way that you get anywhere with Him is by yielding to His will and just holding on to Him. When you are willing to hold on, He is there to help you.

And he said unto him, What is thy name? And he said, Jacob. And he said, Thy name shall be called no more Jacob, but Israel: for as a prince hast thou power with God and with men, and hast prevailed. (Genesis 32:27–28 KJV)

And after this incident, Jacob did have great power both with God and with men.

The principle for power, the formula, is *yielding!* Too many believers go through life today never learning to yield to the will of God in their prayer lives. But God says that if we will be filled with the Holy Spirit and yield to His will in prayer, we will have power with Him and with men. How we need that power today!

ABRAHAM WILL
LEAD US IN PRAYER

THE PRAYERS OF MANY OF GOD'S SAINTS ARE
recorded on the pages of Scripture. They are there for our
instruction and for our help. Paul wrote:

> *For whatever things were written before were written for*
> *our learning, that we through the patience and comfort*
> *of the Scriptures might have hope.* (Romans 15:4 NKJV)

So the prayers are recorded in the Word of God by the Holy
Spirit for our example and to encourage us in the matter of
prayer. In an attempt to strengthen the fabric of faith and
prayer, I think it is beneficial for us to study the great prayers
of Scripture.

One such prayer is the prayer of Abraham. According to
the Scriptures, men began to pray after the death of Abel
and the birth of Seth. In fact, it was after Seth became a
grown man. We read:

And as for Seth, to him also a son was born; and he named him Enosh. Then men began to call on the name of the LORD. (Genesis 4:26 NKJV)

But we do not have a recorded prayer until we get to Abraham, my beloved. As far as I can tell, Noah never went to God and prayed that He would hold back the Flood. You don't find that prayer in Scripture. You might think Noah would have prayed that kind of prayer, but he didn't. He went out and preached that a flood was coming. (See Genesis 6:3 and 1 Peter 3:18–20.)

Abraham's prayer, the first prayer recorded in Scripture, was not a prayer of adoration or praise. It wasn't even a prayer of request or petition to God. This prayer opened with a question mark.

And Abraham came near and said, "Would You also destroy the righteous with the wicked?" (Genesis 18:23 NKJV)

This man Abraham opened his prayer with a dark question. He was a doubting Thomas, if you please. God had told Abraham of His plan to destroy the city of Sodom, but Abraham doubted His decision. So he went to God and asked skeptically, "Would You also destroy the righteous with the wicked?" Abraham felt that God would not be right in destroying a city, no matter how wicked it was, if there were fifty or even ten people in that city who were righteous. But, you see, Abraham didn't know anything about Sodom. As far as we know, he never visited his nephew Lot down there. All he knew was that one day God came to visit him, and He told Abraham that He was going to destroy the cities of Sodom and Gomorrah. And Abraham questioned God.

I say it reverently, my beloved, but it's a good thing God answered that question for Abraham. Again I say this reverently, if God had not answered that question for Abraham, today we may as well bow down before a totem pole as worship a living God in spirit and in truth. Because the answer to this question is very important for Abraham and those coming after him. In fact, God said Himself that it was important for Him to clarify this issue with Abraham.

And the LORD said, "Shall I hide from Abraham what I am doing, since Abraham shall surely become a great and mighty nation, and all the nations of the earth shall be blessed in him? For I have known him, in order that he may command his children and his household after him, that they keep the way of the LORD, to do righteousness and justice, that the LORD may bring to Abraham what He has spoken to him." (Genesis 18:17–19 NKJV)

Abraham thought there must be at least fifty righteous people in Sodom, and he could not understand a righteous God destroying a city with that many people in it. He'd be telling his children that God had not acted righteously, they in turn would tell their children, and by the time it got to us, we'd have a very bad impression of God.

After all, that had happened before. After the Flood, men started getting some peculiar ideas about God. It's my opinion that at the Tower of Babel they worshiped the sun. Do you know why they were worshiping the sun? They said, "The God we've been hearing about sent the clouds and the storm and drowned all of our fathers. We didn't like that. So we worship the sun now. The sun will never send rain."

And this idea they had of God went out from the Tower of Babel and spread so that even more people had that wrong impression of God. Have you ever seen some of the images that they made back then to represent God? They're hideous! That's the kind of god they thought He was. They made Him frightful and horrible and fearful. Why? Because they didn't know Him. After the Flood, they said, "God's awful. We can't understand why He'd destroy so many lovely, fine, cultured people."

My beloved, you're going to have to come to that kind of an interpretation: either God is wonderful or men are wonderful; either God is terrible or men are terrible. The heathen today say that God is terrible and man is wonderful. But the Word of God says God is wonderful, even His name is Wonderful, and men are sinners. You've got to come to that kind of conclusion one way or the other.

So it's a good thing God told Abraham what He was getting ready to do, because Abraham would have come to the wrong conclusion about God. Abraham would have been telling everyone, "You know the God I serve? I've been greatly disappointed. He destroyed the city of Sodom, and you know there must have been fifty righteous people in that city. What do you think of a God who would destroy fifty righteous people?" So God said, "Shall I hide from Abraham that which I'm going to do? No. I'm going to tell him, because he's going to tell his children, and he's to become a blessing to all nations. Generations from now, people will still be talking about Abraham, and I want them to know the truth concerning this situation."

So God said to Abraham:

"Because the outcry against Sodom and Gomorrah is great, and because their sin is very grave, I will go down now and see whether they have done altogether according to the outcry against it that has come to Me; and if not, I will know." Then the men turned away from there and went toward Sodom, but Abraham still stood before the LORD. (Genesis 18:20–22 NKJV)

Abraham was stunned. And after he got his senses back, he looked up to heaven and said, "Would You also destroy the righteous with the wicked?" (Genesis 18:23 NKJV)

What is the first thing that entered Abraham's mind? The first thing that entered his mind, of course, was Lot. He had rescued Lot once, and now Lot was again in danger. I think that Abraham had wondered many times about Lot and his relationship with God, but he at least hoped that

Lot was a saved man. So he asked God, "What about the righteous?" I believe Abraham would have told you that he thought there were many people in the city of Sodom who were saved. He could not understand why God would destroy the righteous with the wicked. What a picture we have here!

How many righteous people ought there be in Sodom before the judgment should be held back? What number would Abraham pick? He hit upon the number of fifty. Notice what he said:

> *Suppose there were fifty righteous within the city; would You also destroy the place and not spare it for the fifty righteous that were in it?* (Genesis 18:24 NKJV)

Now that's a very direct question, is it not? That's doing business with God with figures. "Lord, if there are fifty people who are righteous in the city of Sodom, will you destroy that city? That's what I'd like to know."

> *So the LORD said, "If I find in Sodom fifty righteous within the city, then I will spare all the place for their sakes."* (Genesis 18:26 NKJV)

That's a principle that you can put down. You see, God cannot, nor will He, send a Great Tribulation into the world as a judgment as long as the church is here. Why? He'd be breaking His word and violating one of His principles! May

I say to you, Abraham's ethics were much higher than those of our post-tribulation friends today. They think God is going to send the judgment of the Great Tribulation upon this earth before He takes the church out of this world. When one comes to Christ, he's passed from judgment to life. He's been made righteous in Christ, and God sees him complete in Christ. God cannot judge that one! Judgment fell upon the Savior instead, and He paid the price for us. Therefore, God's final judgment of this world cannot fall as long as the church is still here. That's the principle that's involved here, and it's a very serious principle.

Abraham asked God, "Would You destroy that city if there were fifty righteous people in it?" God answered, "No, I wouldn't." That took the wind right out of Abraham's sails. He had to come up with a new number.

> *"Suppose there were five less than the fifty righteous; would You destroy all of the city for lack of five?" So He said, "If I find there forty-five, I will not destroy it." And he spoke to Him yet again and said, "Suppose there should be forty found there?" So He said, "I will not do it for the sake of forty."* (Genesis 18:28–29 NKJV)

Abraham then countered with "There may be thirty there." And God said, "I'll not do it for the sake of thirty." This man Abraham was "continuing steadfastly in prayer" (Romans 12:12 NKJV). In the Greek, that phrase is a picture of hunting dogs that never let up until they get the animal. I wonder if today we are steadfast in prayer. How many people say, "Oh, I asked God once, and He never answered my prayer"? Abraham stayed with God until he got an answer.

I imagine Abraham said to himself, "Well, wait a minute, maybe the figure was too high. Maybe I better come down." He came down to thirty, then twenty, then ten—continuing steadfastly in prayer. Now the question arises: why didn't Abraham come down below ten? I'll tell you why: at this point he began to doubt Lot's salvation and was afraid that Lot was lost. This disturbed him a great deal, so he was not going to come down any further. But he could have come down to one. He could have said, "Lord, if there is one in that city who is righteous, would You destroy it?" Do you know what God would have said? He would have said, "If there is one who is righteous in that city, I am going to get him out, because I would not destroy a righteous man with the city." How do I know that is the way it would have been? Because that is the way it worked out. There was one righteous man there—Abraham didn't believe it, but God knew him—and that one was Lot.

Candidly, if I were Abraham I would have been unsure about Lot, too. Knowing Lot's life in the city of Sodom, believe me, you couldn't assume for one moment that he was a saved man. Yet if we turn over to 2 Peter, we find assurance that he was indeed saved:

And turning the cities of Sodom and Gomorrah into ashes, [God] condemned them to destruction, making them an example to those who afterward would live ungodly; and delivered righteous Lot, who was oppressed by the filthy conduct of the wicked (for that righteous man, dwelling among them, tormented his righteous soul from day to day by seeing and hearing their lawless deeds). (2 Peter 2:6–8 NKJV)

Lot may have lived in Sodom, but he never was happy. Do you know why? He was God's man, and God's man could never be happy in a place like that. Lot had trusted God, and he had been made righteous. He was acceptable to God. So God got him out of the city. What a wonderful thing to know that you are hidden under Christ, my beloved! When you've trusted Him as Savior, you've "passed from death into life" (John 5:24 NKJV) and shall not come into judgment! What a glorious, wonderful thing that is.

God enjoyed this interview with Abraham. God got great satisfaction out of His man coming to Him and pleading for others. Oh, how God rejoiced in that! He loved to hear Abraham say, "Lord, would You destroy the city for fifty? Oh, maybe I'm just dust and ashes and ought not to say anything, but what about ten? What about ten?" And God delighted in being able to say, "Abraham, for ten I'll not destroy it." God *wants* to save. He rejoices over one sinner that comes to Him. He's put it like this: "For 'whoever calls on the name of the LORD shall be saved'" (Romans 10:13 NKJV).

Popular opinion today says that if you expect God to

answer your prayer, then you must have faith. I hear today that all you have to do is "Just believe!" as if faith were an "Open, sesame" that opens the door to anything you might desire. My friend, don't you know that there is no power in faith itself? Faith can be misplaced and put in the wrong place or in the wrong person. I knew a man years ago in Texas who drilled a wildcat well on his ranch. He believed with all his heart that there was oil there. I never saw any man believe as that man believed. He took his life's savings and poured them into that well, but that's a dry well today. Faith did not make it an oil well. And I have known women to put faith in men who have betrayed them. May I say to you, friends, just to *believe* is not enough. It's *where* your faith is placed and *whom* you believe in that become all-important.

Abraham did not go to God in complete faith. Now don't misunderstand me, Abraham believed in God with all his heart and soul: "For he who comes to God must believe that He is, and that He is a rewarder of those who diligently seek Him" (Hebrews 11:6 NKJV). He believed God heard and answered prayer. But Abraham had some doubts about some matters. So he went to God with it in prayer.

Do you have doubts today? My friend, it's no sin to have doubts. But do not hide them in the closet of your subconscious mind. Do not sweep them under the rug and somehow or another hope that they'll not come out, because they will come out. If you have any doubts, be honest about them and take them to God. We sometimes sing these words:

I must tell Jesus all of my trials,
  I cannot bear these burdens alone;
In my distress He kindly will help me,
  He ever loves and cares for His own.[1]

That's all true, but do we practice it? Do we take our troubles there? Do we take our questions there? Bring your doubts into the sunshine of His presence. Turn up the rocks of doubt and expose the slimy, slithering snakes of your unbelief. Tell Him about it. If you are honest about your doubts and will go to God, you will come to a firm faith the likes of which you've never experienced before.

I say that out of a little experience. I went to a liberal college, and when I went there I promised God that if I ever lost faith in His Word, if I ever lost faith in the Lord Jesus Christ, I'd get out of the ministry. But the time came as a student at that college when my feet were being taken out from under me. I'd never heard before that there was any question about the dating and authorship of the books of the New Testament. But I learned that the liberals have some very serious questions to raise concerning those matters. May I say to you, friends, I found out that I could take my doubts to God. I went to Him and said, "Lord, look here. I can't answer these questions, and unless they're answered for me, I'll have to get out of the ministry." And God put in my hands Adolf Diessmann's book, *Light from the Ancient East*. It is not a fundamental book, but it answered my questions about the authorship and dating of many of the books of the New Testament. May I say to you, that experience brought me to a firmer faith than I'd ever had before. I believe if you've got a doubt and you'll be honest with God about it, He'll see that you beat your music out and come to a firmer faith than you ever had before.

Chapter 6

NEHEMIAH WILL
LEAD US IN PRAYER

NEHEMIAH WAS A MAN OF ACTION AND FEW words. But, unfortunately, this man also left himself open to a great deal of criticism. When God's people went into captivity, God promised that they would be permitted to return to their land at the conclusion of seventy years. It was obviously His will that they return, but when Cyrus gave the decree at the end of seventy years that the Israelites could return to Israel, very few chose to do so. In fact, only about sixty-five thousand of God's people followed His will and returned to the land. The bulk of the nation chose to stay and enjoy the prosperity of the Persian Empire. Nehemiah was one of those who stayed in Persia. He was, therefore, living outside of the will of God.

We can't be too hard on Nehemiah, though. He was born to slaves during the seventy years of captivity, so this man had no tender feelings toward the land of Israel because the only life he'd ever known was in the land of his slavery.

And having been born in a foreign land, he chose a career in government service. We find him pursuing that avocation when we meet him in the first chapter of the Book of Nehemiah.

Nehemiah held a very high position—he was the king's cupbearer. Now when that job was first created, it was merely a headwaiter's job. The cupbearer stood in the presence of the king continually. When anything was brought in to the king for him to eat or drink, the cupbearer would taste it first in order to make sure that the king would not consume anything that was poisoned. So it was a very important and dangerous position for a man to hold. Because the man who held this position had to be so close to the king and carry on a great deal of chitchat back and forth, over time the king came to prefer having a man of ability in the position of cupbearer—someone who could advise and help him. So in time, the office of cupbearer came to correspond to what we in the United States call today the secretary of state. So it was a very high position in the court.

Now, in this position, it would have been easy for Nehemiah to stand aloof from the people of God and the problems that came up after their return to Israel. He could have stood on the sidelines, criticizing and offering them advice. But we find instead that Nehemiah had a holy and heartfelt sympathy for the things of God. Being a layman, he was not up in the land of theory but down in the land of practicality. In other words, the troubles of the Israelites burdened his heart, and he was willing to do something about it. In fact, he wanted to do something very concrete.

I remember hearing a story years ago of a cement contractor who had a reputation in his little town for his love of children. But one time he put down a cement sidewalk, and during the night the kids got into it and each one put his footprint in the wet cement. When the contractor got there the next morning, his sidewalk was all ruined. He was upset and began to issue a tirade against the juvenile delinquents who had ruined his cement. Someone said to him, "But we thought you loved children." He said, "I do love children; I love them in the abstract, but not in the concrete." And, my beloved, Nehemiah was not a man who dealt with things in the abstract. He dealt with that which was concrete, and he believed in *doing* something—even when it came to his prayers.

There are three things I'd like for us to notice about Nehemiah in relation to his prayer life. First of all, there is the solicitude of Nehemiah. Second, the supplication of Nehemiah, and third, the submission of Nehemiah.

SOLICITUDE

One day while Nehemiah was going about his daily duties, he saw a friend of his, Hanani. Hanani was one of those who had returned to Israel, and he had just come from Jerusalem when Nehemiah saw him in the palace. It is during their encounter that we first learn of Nehemiah's solicitude—that is, his concern about the things of God. Nehemiah stopped Hanani and said, "I'm glad to see you, but I'm wondering how things are going at Jerusalem. I have a great burden upon my heart concerning Jerusalem. Would you mind telling me what is happening there?" Hanani shook his head and said:

The survivors who are left from the captivity in the province are there in great distress and reproach. The wall of Jerusalem is also broken down, and its gates are burned with fire. (Nehemiah 1:3 NKJV)

That is not a very pretty picture. What a pitiful spectacle were God's cause and His people!

It would have been very easy for Nehemiah, a layman with a very fine position with the government, to have said, "It's too bad, brother. Sorry to hear it. I'll put you on my prayer list. God bless you." There are many other Christian clichés he could have given. But may I say to you, friends, he wasn't that kind of a man. Notice the effect this news had upon him:

So it was, when I heard these words, that I sat down and wept, and mourned for many days; I was fasting and praying before the God of heaven. (Nehemiah 1:4 NKJV)

What solicitude! When Hanani reported to him the sad condition yonder in Jerusalem, Nehemiah was so concerned that he took time out. He went off and wept, and then he fasted and prayed.

My beloved, I'm convinced that until we get a burden of prayer, we will not see a moving of the Spirit of God in our day. As long as we wear our faith like a light garment that comes off quite easily, God will never move in our midst. If God's people today could only get a burden of prayer!

We don't hear much these days about having a burden of something. I can remember as a boy it was common in that day to talk about a burden of prayer. But we don't want a burden of prayer today. Frankly, we're living in a day when we avoid all the suffering we possibly can. People are afraid to throw themselves into the cause of Christ. After all, they might be called fanatics. But in former years, Christians talked about a "burden of prayer." By that they meant that they were exercised about the things of God, that they didn't do Christian work or perform a service without their hearts being in it.

My beloved, until there comes upon our hearts a burden as there was upon Nehemiah, I don't think God's going to hear and answer our prayers. Because I don't think He believes we really mean business.

But Nehemiah meant business. He held a good position, and it would have been no skin off his nose if things didn't go right at Jerusalem. What should he care about the things yonder in Jerusalem? My friend, he cared everything about it, because the things of God came first with this man. I don't think we would have discovered that had we observed this man at work in the palace of the king. We would have looked at him in his high position in that pagan court and said, "There's certainly nobody in this crowd who is interested in the things of God." But that's because we would be seeing his outward man and not his heart. That man had a breaking heart and a great concern for the things of God.

My friend, does it concern you that there is no spiritual movement today whatsoever? Does it concern you that the world is at its lowest ebb morally? Does it concern you that there is no revival taking place in our day? Is there a burden upon you about these things? If not, maybe what we need to do is pray for a burden. I'm convinced that a great many of us should not ask God to send a revival or to do some great thing. I think we should be asking Him, "Oh, God, put a burden upon my own heart and on my own life. Move upon me, stir me, and put tears in my eyes because of the condition of mankind today. Give me a broken heart over our spiritual condition." It's easy, my beloved, to go through the ritual and the routine, keeping our hearts immune from and inoculated against the great heartache that's about us. Oh, may God lay upon your heart and my heart a real burden for His cause and the things of Christ. Nehemiah had that kind of burden—that solicitude—for the things of God.

SUPPLICATION

Supplication is a special kind of prayer. Paul spoke of it like this:

> *Praying always with all prayer and supplication in the Spirit . . .* (Ephesians 6:18 NKJV)

Supplication is a higher form of prayer. It's a prayer in which the Holy Spirit of God moves and controls the one praying so that he does not pray beyond the will of God. Nehemiah uttered a prayer of supplication. Remember, he was a layman; he never studied the theology of prayer in seminary, so it wasn't a polished prayer. He didn't start off with a note of thanksgiving and praise, followed by the body of the prayer, and then a conclusion. He was just a layman with a great burden, so he simply went to God and opened up his heart to Him about it. He didn't cover all the major points of doctrine, but he sure did pray from his heart.

Notice how he began:

I pray, LORD God of heaven, O great and awesome God . . . (Nehemiah 1:5 NKJV)

Nehemiah did not come to God in this buddy-buddy method that we hear in prayers today. Candidly, I'm not sure we should even use the word *You* in speaking to God. I think we need to reserve all of the dignity and reverence that we possibly can. You don't buddy-up with God in prayer, my beloved. May I say to you, He's high and holy and lifted up. When we get to heaven, no one is going to pat Him on the back and say, "We're sure glad to be here with You." My friend, the minute you and I get to heaven we're going to get down on our knees before Him in adoration and worship, and I can't find any Scripture that says we'll ever get up off of them. There ought to be a reverence in our hearts for God, my beloved!

Nehemiah recognized the necessity of reverence. He did not go before God to trifle. He said:

> *You who keep Your covenant and mercy with those who love You and observe Your commandments . . .*
> (Nehemiah 1:5 NKJV)

He knew that God was far above him, yet this man Nehemiah also knew that God would listen if he poured out his heart to Him. But that doesn't mean this was just a little prayer that Nehemiah tossed off in a moment of emotion. This was his heart's prayer.

> *. . . Please let Your ear be attentive and Your eyes open, that You may hear the prayer of Your servant which I pray before You now, day and night . . .*

As he went around the palace performing his duties and tasks, this prayer was coming continually, not audibly from his mouth, but from his heart.

> *. . . For the children of Israel Your servants, and confess the sins of the children of Israel which we have sinned against You. Both my father's house and I have sinned.*
> (Nehemiah 1:6 NKJV)

Notice Nehemiah's wording in this prayer. Did he say, "I come to confess the sins which *they* have sinned"? No. He confessed the sins "which *we* have sinned against You." Then this man really nailed it down: "I am a sinner. My father's house has sinned. The nation has sinned." How many times do we hear that kind of a confession of sin in our churches? Not very often. But my beloved, when we come to God on that kind of basis, He hears.

Nehemiah continued in prayer:

We have acted very corruptly against You, and have not kept the commandments, the statutes, nor the ordinances which You commanded Your servant Moses.
(Nehemiah 1:7 NKJV)

We can see from this verse that Nehemiah knew and believed God's Word. He rested in it. He was concerned because God's commandments were being ignored.

My beloved, then Nehemiah laid hold of the promise of God. He reminded God of the promise He'd made:

Remember, I pray, the word that You commanded Your servant Moses, saying, "If you are unfaithful, I will scatter you among the nations; but if you return to Me, and keep My commandments and do them, though some of you were cast out to the farthest part of the heavens, yet I will gather them from there, and bring them to the

place which I have chosen as a dwelling for My name."
(Nehemiah 1:8–9 NKJV)

In other words, Nehemiah said, "You promised us that if we disobeyed, You'd scatter us. You've done that. But You also said that if we turned and came back to You, You would regather us and put us back in the land. And now, oh, God, I appeal to You on the basis of Your promise that You'll return us to the land, build up Jerusalem, rebuild the temple, and again make it a great religious center where the nations of the world can turn to You."

My friend, may I say to you that you can never get so close to God as when you are claiming His promises. You can even be saved by just claiming His promise. Our Lord said, "He who hears My word and believes in Him who sent Me has everlasting life, and shall not come into judgment, but has passed from death into life" (John 5:24 NKJV). My friend, you have a right to claim that promise and hold God to it. In fact, He wants you to. How He loved this prayer of Nehemiah. Why? Because Nehemiah held Him to His promise.

SUBMISSION

Now Nehemiah didn't leave it there. He had to *act* upon his prayer. That brings us to the submission of Nehemiah.

You and I sometimes pray for something, and then we go off and forget about it. But God expects us to *do* something about our prayer. He expects our lives and our actions to be toward the answering of our prayer.

Have you ever prayed that a particular person might be saved? If you have, then let me ask you a question: have you ever invited that person to attend church with you? I hear people pray, "Oh, God, move in our midst and save souls." But how can He save them if you and I do not bring them? You see, there is a great deal of praying today that's not backed up by a life of submission to God. Our Lord looked out yonder from the fields white unto harvest, and He said to His disciples, "Therefore pray the Lord of the harvest to send out laborers into His harvest" (Matthew 9:38 NKJV). Later He said, "But go rather to the lost sheep of the house of Israel" (Matthew 10:6 NKJV). Believe me, He never told anyone to pray to whom He didn't also say, "Go. Get busy. Do something about the prayer that you're praying."

Nehemiah did something about his prayer. Let me paraphrase what happened: after praying that God would restore Jerusalem and make it the religious center again, Nehemiah then went into the presence of the king. We know that Nehemiah must have been a very pleasant and joyful person, because on this particular day he was unusually sorrowful and the king noticed it. The king stopped the state business and said, "Nehemiah, what's on your heart? You didn't stay home from work, so you must not be sick. Evidently you have a sorrow in your heart. What is it?" So Nehemiah shot up a prayer to the God of heaven. It was a brief prayer, and I imagine it was something like, "Oh, Lord, help me say the right thing." Then he said to the king, "Sir, how can I be happy when the city of my fathers lies waste and the temple is in ruins? How can I be joyful when God's name is not being elevated and He's not being honored? Do you mind if I take a leave of absence? I don't want just to sit here on the sidelines; I want to go up yonder to Jerusalem and do something about it." (See Nehemiah 2:1–6.) The king granted him a leave of absence, and Nehemiah went to Jerusalem. And when he got there he rallied the forces and led in the rebuilding of the wall of Jerusalem. In fact, this man was raised up by God to encourage His people. You see, he didn't just stay down on his knees, praying. He did something about his prayer.

How we need Nehemiah's kind of prayer today, my beloved! We need solicitude for the things of God. Then we need real prayer—prayer that comes from a burdened heart. And then, my beloved, we need to pray the kind of prayer that leads to action. Our lives should demonstrate that we have submitted to our own prayers and that we mean business with God. God hears and answers prayers like that.

Chapter 7

THE CHURCH WILL
LEAD US IN PRAYER

BETWEEN THE OLD TESTAMENT AND THE NEW Testament there is a grand canyon of silence spanning four hundred years. It is a chasm of time during which heaven was completely silent. After Malachi spoke at the close of the Old Testament, there was no further word from God. It is a void that God did not attempt to fill with any new message from Himself. But when the New Testament finally opens, we find ourselves in an entirely different climate and atmosphere from the one in the Old Testament. In a very definite sense, all things have become new.

We find, first of all, that a Savior has come, died upon a cross, been buried, and then risen from the dead. That was such an important event in history that even the calendars of the world were arranged and adjusted around it. We also discover that a new group has come into existence—the church. The church is not found anywhere in the Old Testament, but when we come to the New Testament we find the church for the first time.

Prayer also is made new in the New Testament. Our Lord prepared His disciples for it in the Upper Room discourse, and what He had to say is vital for us today:

> *Most assuredly, I say to you, whatever you ask the Father in My name He will give you. Until now you have asked nothing in My name* [that is, no one had ever before prayed in His name]. *Ask, and you will receive, that your joy may be full.* (John 16:23–24 NKJV)

May I say, that changed everything! Now the child of God is to pray *to* the Father *in the name of* the Lord Jesus *by the power of* the Holy Spirit. You may be wondering, *Aren't we to pray directly to the Lord Jesus?* I don't think so. Is it wrong? No, I don't think it's wrong. The Lord Jesus is God, and He is capable of hearing prayer. But today He is seated at the right hand of the Father in the position of our Intercessor. When we go directly to Him, we rob ourselves of the most wonderful Intercessor there is. We are to ask of the Father in the name of His Son.

Prayer is the very heart, blood, and heartbeat of the church. In fact, the church was born in a prayer meeting! We read:

> *When the Day of Pentecost had fully come, they were all with one accord in one place.* (Acts 2:1 NKJV)

"With one accord" means that they were together in prayer, my beloved, when the Holy Spirit came upon them, marking the beginning of the church.

The prayers of the early church were potent and powerful—they shook walls and loosened prison doors! Unfortunately, prayer in the church today is impotent, anemic, and sickly. Someone could argue that the church of today is not the same as the church of the first century. I heartily agree. The church of the first century was the apostolic church; the church of today is the apostate church. Then it was the persecuted church; today it's the petulant and petted church. Then the church was united; today it is divided. Then the church was warm and spiritual; today it is cold and materialistic. Then it was young and virile; today it is old and decrepit. The early church was committed to Christ; the church today is comfortable in the world. The church at the beginning was a church of conviction; the church today is marked by confusion. The church then had confession; today it has compromise. Then it was a church marked by consistency; today it is a church of contradiction. I'll say there's a difference between the church of the first century and the church today!

But may I say to you, the early church is still a lesson and an incentive to us in the present day, especially when it comes to the matter of prayer. If you want to get acquainted with the members of the early church, read their prayers. You will find out what kind of men and women they were by looking at the prayers that they uttered to God. Their prayers thrill my heart, and they hold valuable lessons for us today.

CONSCIOUSNESS OF DANGER

The first thing I notice is that the consciousness of danger caused the members of the early church to be united in prayer. Let us turn again to the Book of Acts:

> *And when they had entered, they went up into the upper room where they were staying . . . These all continued with one accord in prayer and supplication.* (Acts 1:13–14 NKJV)

After the ascension of our Lord, these people were frightened. So they came together and met in an upper room. Why did they meet in a secret place? For the simple reason that dangers lurked outside, and these men and women were afraid. But rather than make them scatter, their fear caused them to come together and unite in prayer.

After the Day of Pentecost, these people of God were threatened again—this time in the form of persecution. Peter and John were arrested because "they taught the people and preached in Jesus the resurrection from the dead" (Acts 4:2 NKJV). After they were released from prison we read:

> *And being let go, they went to their own companions and reported all that the chief priests and elders had said to them. So when they heard that, they raised their voice to God with one accord and said: "Lord, You are God, who made heaven and earth and the sea, and all that is in them."* (Acts 4:23–24 NKJV)

Later on in their prayer they said to the Lord, "Now, Lord, look on their threats" (Acts 4:29 NKJV). They were being threatened. May I say again, it was their consciousness of danger that caused them to be united in prayer.

CONVICTION CONCERNING THE SOVEREIGNTY OF GOD

The second thing I'd like to note is that they had a conviction concerning the sovereignty of God. This is an hour when God's people need to be mastered by God. So many people talk about God's will and how they want to be in it. But what *is* God's will for most people today? A lot of folk think following His will means getting God to vote along with them on what they want to do. My friend, we need today to have a conviction concerning the sovereignty of the almighty God.

That word *conviction* is an interesting word. From that same stem comes the word *convict*. A convict is someone who has been put inside of a penitentiary, had a number slapped on his back, and been shut up behind bars. He can't even move without someone telling him he can! Friends, whether we like it or not, you and I need to have a conviction. We need to be convicts of God, doing His will the way He dictates.

Returning to our example of the early church, notice that it says, "So when they heard that" (Acts 4:24 NKJV). What was it that they'd heard? Well, the Sanhedrin told Peter and John that they were no longer to preach in the name of Jesus (see Acts 4:18). If they persisted in teaching about Jesus, they would be arrested again and then put to death. In other words, witnessing in the name of Jesus would have been a death sentence. But notice how they reacted to this news:

> *So when they heard that, they raised their voice to God with one accord and said: "Lord, You are God."* (Acts 4:24 NKJV)

I want to pause for just a moment to examine that word *Lord*. Our translation fails to bring out the real meaning of it. The word used here is not the same Greek word translated elsewhere in the New Testament as "Lord." The word used in Acts 4:24 is an altogether different word. In the Greek, it is *despotes*. Does that sound familiar? Maybe you're thinking that it sounds like a very terrible word in English: despot. Well, that's what *despotes* is. Our God is a despot; He is the greatest dictator that there's ever been. What I mean by that is simply this: there is no will that's going to prevail except His. Our God is in total control of this universe. That's why the early church prayed, "Lord, You are God. You are the absolute dictator."

Not only did these people recognize God's sovereignty, but they also recognized that He is the Creator.

> *You are God, who made heaven and earth and the sea, and all that is in them.* (Acts 4:24 NKJV)

Friends, until you and I are convinced that God is the Creator, we'll never pray aright to God. You see, this just happens to be *His* universe. He never consulted me or anyone else when He made it. In fact, up to the present moment He has never consulted any of us on any matter at all. And it's just too bad if we don't like it, because God is not running this universe to suit us—He's running this universe to suit Himself.

The world today rejects that which is spiritual and supernatural, and therefore they deny that there is a Creator. But the early church was aware that there is a spiritual beyond the material and a power back of the physical. So when they went to God in prayer, they recognized Him as the Creator. And, my friend, real prayer is impossible for anyone who denies that God is the Creator and that He is sovereign.

CONVICTION CONCERNING THE SCRIPTURES

Continuing in their prayer, the members of the early church revealed something else about themselves: they had a conviction concerning the Scriptures. That is a tremendous lesson to us today.

> *. . . Who by the mouth of Your servant David have said, "Why did the nations rage, and the people plot vain things? The kings of the earth took their stand, and the rulers were gathered together against the LORD and against His Christ."* (Acts 4:25–26 NKJV)

They were quoting Psalm 2. The liberal critic today says that David did not write that psalm. But the early church believed that David *did* write it *by* the Holy Spirit *about* the Messiah. They also believed that the fulfillment of David's psalm began when Jesus Christ was crucified:

> *For truly against Your holy Servant Jesus, whom You anointed, both Herod* [the representative of the nation Israel] *and Pontius Pilate* [the representative of the Roman Empire]*, with the Gentiles and the people of Israel, were gathered together.* (Acts 4:27 NKJV)

Now this raises a question: who put Christ to death? Actually, in a very real sense, all of us are implicated in that murder. If we were not sinners, Christ would never have died on the cross. But on another plane, the nation Israel is responsible for His death. And in another sense the Roman government is responsible, for He was crucified on a Roman cross.

But the important thing to notice is what these people prayed, for this is the most amazing thing about it all. On the Day of Pentecost, Peter went before the people and said, "You're guilty of murder! You killed Him!" (See Acts 2:22–24.) But later when they entered into private prayer, they said something else to God:

> *. . . To do whatever Your hand and Your purpose determined before to be done.* (Acts 4:28 NKJV)

They didn't go to God and say, "Lord, the Gentiles came together with the nation Israel and murdered Your Son." They didn't say that at all. They said, "Lord, You're sovereign, and the reason this happened is because it is according to Your will. They came together to put Jesus to death because You determined it." You see, believing in what God has promised in the Scriptures and recognizing His sovereignty are essential to understanding His will.

Our prayers today are filled with our own wants and not the will of God. My friend, prayer is not a method of trying to get something from God that He's reluctant to give. Prayer is a mighty, transforming experience whereby you and I are brought under the mighty hand of a sovereign God! And whatever comes to us today, we can face it and say, "This has come by the will of God, and I accept it."

CONSISTENT AND COURAGEOUS IN THE PRESENCE OF PERSECUTION

There is one more lesson I'd like to glean from this prayer: the people of the early church were courageous in the presence of persecution. Listen to them:

> *Now, Lord, look on their threats, and grant to Your servants that with all boldness they may speak Your word.*
> (Acts 4:29 NKJV)

They did not pray to be delivered from their persecution. May I say to you, this shows that they were consistent. Don't misunderstand me—when I use the word *consistent* I do not mean it in the sense of doing or saying the exact same thing yesterday, today, and forever. What is it to be consistent, then? Being consistent means simply this: to be mastered by and guided by great principles and then sticking to them regardless of the hardships that might come up. And the people of the early church did just that. They had a star by which they sailed their little bark, and they never departed from it. Do you know what it was? It was the will and glory of God. That's all they were interested in.

They may not have asked to be delivered from persecution, but they did ask for something else. You see, they were filled with fear—fear that they might fail God. That ought to be our fear as well, my beloved—fear that we'll fail Him. And so they asked God for courage. They said, "Our trouble is that we're afraid of failing You! So give us boldness." They needed courage to be able to go forward and continue doing God's will, so they simply asked for it. Oh, how we need to do that today.

Let me acknowledge that some may be thinking, *But the people of the early church were supersaints; we are not. They belonged to a race above us. These people practically had halos about their heads!* No, they didn't, my beloved. They were "men of like passions" (Acts 14:15 KJV) as we are.

Let me give you an example. We are told in Acts 12 that when Peter was in prison, the church met together and prayed earnestly for God to deliver him. And God did—those prison doors were shaken and Peter was freed. So he went over and knocked on the door where the church was assembled and praying for his deliverance. But did they have faith? May I say, they had none whatsoever. A little serving maid by the name of Rhoda went to the door, saw that it was Simon Peter, and ran back to tell everyone. She didn't even stop to open the door and let Peter in. But do you know, the church didn't believe her! They said, "It couldn't possibly be Simon Peter." Well, why not? They'd been in there praying for his deliverance, hadn't they? Yes, but they didn't believe very much.

It is a great comfort to me that the early church, with all its tremendous spiritual power, on this occasion did not believe that their prayers had been answered. Isn't the same thing true of us? When we have an answer to prayer, we rejoice and talk about it as if we are surprised. Honestly, we really didn't expect an answer. Yet God heard and answered anyway. How gracious He is!

Today we need to lay hold of the power of the early church's prayers. What was their secret? Simply this: they were filled with the Holy Spirit. Look at what happened at the conclusion of their prayer:

> *And when they had prayed, the place where they were assembled together was shaken; and they were all filled with the Holy Spirit, and they spoke the word of God with boldness.* (Acts 4:31 NKJV)

There are some who argue that this was a second Pentecost. It was nothing of the kind. There has only been one Pentecost, and it was mentioned earlier in Acts 2: "When the Day of Pentecost had fully come" (Acts 2:1 NKJV). That day never did end. In fact, we're living in it today. This is the age of grace when God regenerates and makes new creatures out of every sinner that comes to Christ. You see, all things became new in the New Testament. The Holy Spirit today indwells every believer, but the thing we're told to do now is to be *filled* with the Holy Spirit. When we, as new creations, are filled with the Holy Spirit of God, He will give us what we need to face all of our persecutions and all of our fears. We cannot face life today without the supernatural power of the Holy Spirit. That is the secret to powerful prayer.

JAMES WILL
LEAD US IN PRAYER

THE BIBLE RECORDS SEVERAL MEN BY THE NAME of James. So we ought to identify and introduce the James that we have in mind, and that is the one who wrote the Epistle of James. This James was our Lord's flesh-and-blood brother. He was a son of Mary and Joseph, which made him a half brother of the Lord Jesus. We find a reference to him in the Gospel of Mark:

> *Is this not the carpenter, the Son of Mary, and brother of James, Joses, Judas, and Simon? And are not His sisters here with us?* (Mark 6:3)

I believe it was this same James whom Paul referred to in his epistle to the Galatians:

> *And when James, Cephas, and John, who seemed to be pillars, perceived the grace that had been given to me,*

they gave me and Barnabas the right hand of fellowship, that we should go to the Gentiles and they to the circumcised. (Galatians 2:9 NKJV)

This James is the man who we believe is the author of the Epistle of James.

His epistle opens with this:

James, a bondservant of God and of the Lord Jesus Christ . . . (James 1:1 NKJV)

I do not know about you, but I am confident that if I had been the Lord's half brother on the human side, somewhere in this epistle I would let the reader know it. I would have brought in that fact in a very casual and humble way, but I surely would have let you know. However, James did not do that. Instead, he called himself a bond slave of God and of the Lord Jesus Christ.

Our Lord Jesus was so human here on this earth that even His own brethren did not believe at first. They had been brought up with Him and seen Him grow up. They may have noticed that He was unusual, but they did not believe He was the Savior of the world. Of course, your family members are always the hardest people to reach; yet they are the ones we should reach. James came to know the Lord Jesus not only as his blood brother but as his own Savior, and then he became His bond slave. Notice what James called Him—he used His full name, the Lord Jesus Christ.

James said, "He is my Lord." Jesus was His human name, and James knew Him as Jesus, his half brother; but he also knew Him as Christ, the Messiah who had come and died for the sins of the world.

In studying this epistle, we find that James's outlook on life was a little different from ours. The fact of the matter is that he seemed to have nothing in common with the contemporary Christianity that we know today. I do not believe he would have very much to do with this frivolous and sophisticated type of fundamentalism that we have about us today. He was austere, rugged, serious, and solemn. He was also very practical. He believed that Christianity had to be put in shoe leather, and if you couldn't put it in shoe leather then it wasn't true Christianity. So he was very pragmatic, but he was also a man of prayer. And as I've mentioned before, tradition says that he was known as "Old Camel-Knees" in the early church because he spent so much time on his knees in prayer. So he is a great man to turn to for practical lessons on the subject of prayer.

The subject of his epistle is the ethics of Christianity, not doctrine or works as many seem to think. He was discussing faith—a faith that works, my beloved. So he gave to us the skills and techniques necessary for living the Christian life faithfully. And in that he had a great deal to say about prayer. In fact, he made three practical suggestions in the area of prayer, where you and I live and move and have our being: prayer and wisdom, prayer and worldliness, and prayer and wellness.

PRAYER AND WISDOM

When James spoke of wisdom, he meant it in relation to the trials and troubles of this life. He was not talking about book learning or anything philosophical. Remember, James was practical, and everything he talked about in this epistle was, likewise, very practical. He was talking here about having wisdom regarding God's will for our lives. Look at what he said:

> *My brethren, count it all joy when you fall into various trials, knowing that the testing of your faith produces patience. But let patience have its perfect work, that you may be perfect and complete, lacking nothing.* (James 1:2–4 NKJV)

When James talked about being perfect, what he was saying was that you and I as Christians should be complete and fully mature. In order to do that, we need to know God's will and stay in it. But following God's will requires making certain decisions. James wasn't referring to just one great decision for life, but he was talking about the many daily decisions that you and I have to make—decisions concerning very practical things. Shall we go here? Or shall we do that? Shall we refrain from doing this? Now, these are the things James was saying should be the matter of prayer in order to determine God's will. That's the only way we'll ever become well-rounded, mature Christians.

If we need wisdom in order to make decisions about the things that come up each day, just what are we to do when we are unsure of God's will concerning our lives? James gave us a very practical answer: we're to ask God. He said:

> *If any of you lacks wisdom, let him ask of God, who gives to all liberally and without reproach, and it will be given to him.* (James 1:5 NKJV)

You see, it's the everyday decisions in life that take many of us out of the will of God. Many of us probably start out in the morning in the will of God, but before we come to high noon we've moved out of the will of God. The reason is because we were confronted with decisions to be made, and we thought they didn't need to be taken to God in prayer. But may I say to you, to know God's will we should be constantly in touch with Him, asking Him for His will concerning these matters.

Decisions face us constantly, and these decisions are disturbing to many folk. I recall a story about a boy who got a job in a country store. The proprietor sent him down to the basement to sort potatoes. He said to the boy, "I want you to put all the big potatoes on this side of the basement and all the small potatoes on the other side of the basement. Be very careful with this—the big potatoes over here and the small potatoes over there." The boy said, "Yes, sir," and he got to work.

After about two hours had passed, he came upstairs and said to his boss, "I'm quitting." So the proprietor said to him,

"Son, you haven't worked but just a little while. Is the work too hard for you?" The boy answered, "No, sir. The work's not too hard." The proprietor tried again, "Am I not paying you enough?" And the boy said, "Yes, you're paying me enough, sir." So the proprietor asked the boy, "Well, what is it that's wrong?" The boy said, "It's all them decisions I have to make." May I say to you, my beloved, that's the problem with life today: it's them decisions that we have to make. We've all come to places where we couldn't tell the big potatoes from the small potatoes.

There are many times in our lives when we are faced with a decision and we don't have the wisdom to know which way we should turn. Imagine a Christian who sincerely wants to do God's will. But what *is* God's will for his life? He moves out into today and tomorrow and next week, saying, "I want to do God's will." But he comes to the crossroads of life and two ways open up to him, one to the right hand and one to the left hand. Which way shall he go? God has not put up a marker at the crossroads. He hasn't put up a signal light there that turns green for Go and red for *Stop*. He hasn't sent an audible voice out of heaven that says to us, "This is the way, walk ye in it." Which way are we to go, my beloved, when we come to places like that in our lives? We do not know which way to turn, and the others are blowing their horns and saying to us, "Move on!" And, friends, in life we've got to move on. But what decision shall we make?

James said, "If any man lacks wisdom, let him ask God." God is not stingy in this department—He is generous! If we

look to Him for wisdom in these matters, He gives to everyone liberally. I can speak only for myself, but the highway I've
come on hasn't been marked very well. I've come to many
crossroads without knowing which way to turn. But I believe,
my beloved, that God moves us to these crossroads purposely.
If He gave us a clear road map, we'd forever be looking at that
road map and not be looking to Him. So He doesn't always
make it clear. That keeps us close to Him, you see. But if you
and I will look to Him for wisdom, He'll let us move out.

My beloved, you and I need wisdom. And if we are willing to commit matters in our lives to Him, God will lead
and guide us. That doesn't mean that all in life will go
smoothly. Many have difficulty. And somebody is sure to
say, "But I might make a mistake and choose the wrong
path." Maybe you will. Paul almost made a mistake, but the
Holy Spirit prevented him from making it. Look at what
happened on Paul's second missionary journey:

> *Now when they had gone through Phrygia and the
> region of Galatia, they were forbidden by the Holy Spirit
> to preach the word in Asia.* (Acts 16:6 NKJV)

At that time, Ephesus was the capital of the province of
Asia. Later, Paul would do his greatest missionary work in
Ephesus. But at this time when Paul wanted to go there, the
Spirit of God stopped him and blocked the way. Well, if
Paul's way to Ephesus was blocked, he should have known
then which way God wanted him to go, right? But he didn't.

After they had come to Mysia, they tried to go into Bithynia, but the Spirit did not permit them. (Acts 16:7 NKJV)

Paul thought, *Well, if the Spirit of God doesn't intend for me to go south, He certainly intends for me to go north into Bithynia.* But the Spirit of God blocked him again and said, "Not this way."

You see, God doesn't flash green lights for us. So we need wisdom to make these decisions that confront us in life. God didn't put steering wheels on any of us for a reason—*He* wants to steer us! So when we come to the crossroads, we have a right to look to Him and ask for wisdom if we mean to do His will. And if we do take the wrong fork, that will be made clear. This is very practical. This is putting your prayers into shoe leather.

PRAYER AND WORLDLINESS

What is worldliness? I believe the average Christian in our so-called fundamental churches would give one of several answers. Some would say worldliness is a matter of the kind of amusements you attend or indulge in. Others would say it is the kind of crowd you run with. Still others would say worldliness is a matter of the conversation you engage in or the way you dress. That is what many today would call worldliness. James would not agree. He said:

Where do wars and fights come from among you? Do they not come from your desires for pleasure that war in your members? You lust and do not have. You murder and covet and cannot obtain. You fight and war. Yet you do not have because you do not ask [pray]. (James 4:1–2 NKJV)

May I say to you, that's worldliness—strife and envy. The spirit of the world today is a spirit of strife and competition. James said that the worldly have a desire to get, and they are willing to hurt and harm to get it. We go so far today as to build missiles and nuclear weapons in order to get what we want. That's the spirit of the world today.

The worst thing that can happen is when that spirit of strife and competition gets into the heart of a believer. That is what makes a worldly Christian. God has made the heart so that only He can fill it. Even when we attempt to put the whole world in it, the heart's not filled and still longs for more. That spirit of wanting more, that spirit of getting, leads to carnality. That's the thing that Paul spoke about when he wrote to the Corinthians:

And I, brethren, could not speak to you as to spiritual people but as to carnal, as to babes in Christ. I fed you with milk and not with solid food; for until now you were not able to receive it, and even now you are still not able; for you are still carnal. For where there are envy, strife, and divisions among you, are you not carnal and behaving like mere men? (1 Corinthians 3:1–3 NKJV)

When that spirit of strife comes into the heart, it makes a carnal Christian.

But notice what James said:

You ask and do not receive, because you ask [pray] **amiss, that you may spend it on your pleasures.** (James 4:3 NKJV)

The reason that our prayers are not answered is because our prayers are selfish. They are not for God's glory, but they are for our own desires, our own lusts, our own pleasures. For that reason, we must examine our prayers to see if they are genuine and to understand why we maybe didn't get the answers that we asked for. Do we pray because we have a bad case of "gimmes"? Or is it because we really want God's glory done?

He prayed for strength that he might achieve;
    He was made weak that he might obey.
He prayed for health that he might do greater things;
    He was given infirmity that he might do better things.
He prayed for riches that he might be happy;
    He was given poverty that he might be wise.
He prayed for power that he might have the praise of men;
    He was given infirmity that he might feel the need of God.
He prayed for all things that he might enjoy life;
    He was given life that he might enjoy all things.
He had received nothing that he asked for—all that he hoped for;
    His prayer was answered—he was most blessed.[1]

James said that prayer works, and if our prayers are not working it's because we're praying as worldly Christians.

Why do we want it? Why are we asking for it? Is it because we have in our hearts the spirit of the world? My beloved, worldliness is the thing that will short-circuit the power line of prayer quicker than anything else.

PRAYER AND WELLNESS

The problem of keeping well physically is one of the greatest problems that we have. In fact, that's the way we greet each other, is it not? We meet somebody and say, "How are you?" I remember as a boy in southern Oklahoma, I used to know a dear little old lady. You'd ask her, "How do you feel this morning, Miss So-and-So?" And it was either one of two things: she'd say, "I feel pert" or "I feel puny." She seemed to feel puny more often than she felt pert. A great many of us are that way. We want to enjoy good health, and we feel like we ought to have good health. We reason it like this: "I can be a better Christian, I can do more for God, if I am well. Therefore it must be God's will for me to stay well." If you say that it is God's will for every Christian who gets sick to be healed, you must agree that the logical conclusion of that line of thinking is that the Christian will never die. He will be healed of every disease that causes death. May I say, that is ridiculous. Saying that it is God's will for all to be well and all to be healed is a cruel hoax perpetrated upon simple believers.

James understood that it must be the will of God in order for someone to be healed, and I agree with him. But, again,

James was very practical, and he had for us practical suggestions on what we should do when we are not well.

> *Is anyone among you suffering? Let him pray. Is anyone cheerful? Let him sing psalms. Is anyone among you sick? Let him call for the elders of the church, and let them pray over him, anointing him with oil in the name of the Lord. And the prayer of faith will save the sick, and the Lord will raise him up. And if he has committed sins, he will be forgiven.* (James 5:13–15 NKJV)

James was not actually asking a question here. He was saying, "Someone is sick among you." What are you to do? One thing he suggested was "anointing him with oil in the name of the Lord." There are several words that are translated "anoint" in the New Testament. One of them is used in a religious sense; that word is *chrio* in the Greek. It means to anoint with some scented unguent or oil. It is a sacred word, and it is used to refer to the anointing of Christ by God the Father with the Holy Spirit. Another word translated "anoint" is *aleipho*. It has nothing to do with ceremony or religion at all. It is used a number of times in the New Testament. In Matthew 6:17 (NKJV) we read, "But you, when you fast, anoint your head and wash your face." That use of "anoint" is cosmetic—it means simply to put something on to improve your looks. "Anoint" is used again in the Old Testament to describe putting medicine on a boil Hezekiah had on his body. So it is also used as a medical term. There's no religious value in that use of the word at all.

Now which word for "anoint" is used in James? Well, it's the medical word. It has nothing in the world to do with religious ceremony at all. It is a mistaken idea to say that this refers to some religious ceremony of putting a little oil from a bottle on someone's head, as if that would have some healing merit in it. As it is used here in James, the act of anointing has no mystical merit whatsoever. James was too practical for that. What he referred to in James 5:14 was medication. When you are sick, you are to take the medications and seek out the doctors that are available to help make you well.

But remember, James was also a man of prayer. He said, "Call for the elders to pray." I believe we ought to have more prayer for the sick. I think that it is God's will that we pray for the sick. James made this very clear:

And the prayer of faith will save the sick, and the Lord will raise him up. And if he has committed sins, he will be forgiven. (James 5:15 NKJV)

"And the prayer of faith shall save the sick." I believe you are to call on God's people to pray for you when you are sick. That does not mean God will automatically heal you. But if it is in His will, you will be made well.

I wish I could say to you that I know by daily experience, moment by moment, what it is to be completely submerged in the will of God. I'm sorry to report that many times I've held back and not been fully in God's will. But I am prepared to say this: I've been in that paradise several times. I've looked over the fence into that wonderful, marvelous garden where He wants us to walk today in shoe leather. Where you can commit your way and your will to Him completely! Where you can go out and face the world, saying, "I belong to Him. I may not know what to do tomorrow morning, but I'm committing it to Him. And if you see me stumble and fall, I want you to know I'm going to get up and brush myself off and try the other way. Because I'm committed to Him. And if I get sick I'm going to Him in prayer, asking Him to make me well. Then I'm going to call the doctor. And if I don't get well, I'll know I have His will. And it will be the best thing in the world for me."

Do you need wisdom about God's will in order to make the decisions of life? Go to God in prayer. He hears, and He gives liberally. Do you have a spirit of strife within your heart today? Maybe that's what short-circuited your prayer. Do you want to be well? Every normal person wants to be well. Can we make that a matter of prayer? We certainly can. And James said that you can expect an answer from God if you do pray about it.

WHEN
PAUL PRAYED

IT'S INTERESTING THAT WE DON'T OFTEN THINK
of Paul as an outstanding man of prayer. When you think of
anyone excelling in any field of service in the early church,
Paul the apostle must be up toward the top. We would put
him at the top of the list as a great missionary of the cross,
and we can't think of any greater example of apostleship
than Paul. If we were to make a list of ten of the greatest
preachers of the church, we would certainly put Paul as
number one. He was also one of the greatest teachers. The
Lord Jesus was, of course, the greatest of all—"No man ever
spoke like this Man!" (John 7:46 NKJV)—and Paul certainly
followed in that tradition. He is also an example of a good
pastor. According to Dr. Luke, Paul wept with the believers
at Ephesus when he took leave of them. He loved them, and
they loved him.

But how about being representative of a great man of
prayer—would you put Paul on that list? We think of Moses

yonder on Mount Sinai interceding for the children of Israel. We think of David with his psalms and the confession of his awful sin. We think of Elijah who stood alone before an altar drenched with water at Mount Carmel. Then there was Daniel who opened his window toward Jerusalem and prayed every day even though he lived in a hostile land under a hostile power. The Lord Jesus was the Man of prayer, so much so that one of His disciples asked Him, "Lord, teach us to pray" (Luke 11:1 NKJV). But did you know that Paul was also a great man of prayer? With all of his other qualities, we seldom think of Paul as a man of *prayer*, yet this is the field in which he excelled, I believe, above all others.

When I was teaching in the Bible Institute of Los Angeles, I would ask the students during their studies of Paul's epistles to make a list of all his prayers. They were to put down every time Paul said he was praying for someone. Lo and behold, student after student would come to me and say, "I had no idea Paul had such a prayer list. I didn't know he prayed for so many people!" Paul was a great man of prayer.

Years ago there was a preacher in Dallas, Texas, who was not a great preacher, but he had a great church and a great ministry—because his was largely a ministry of prayer. He wrote his prayer list on a roll of paper from an adding machine! When he unrolled it, it went through the living room, into the dining room, and on into the kitchen. When this man started praying down that list, the officers in his church could always tell it, because he would call this one and that one on the phone and say, "Look, I'm praying for So-and-So, and he hasn't accepted Christ yet. Would you go over and talk to him while I pray for him?" The officers would always say, "Well, we know that Dr. Anderson is praying because he has us all working." May I say to you, he had a great ministry because he had a great prayer life. By the way, what kind of prayer list do you have? How many people do you remember in prayer, even once a week? Maybe you are living a busy life these days, but once a week do you take time out to go down a list and remember specific people in prayer?

Paul the apostle is, in my opinion, the man God has given to the believer as the great example to follow when praying. The Epistle to the Ephesians records two of Paul's prayers. In chapter one, having set before us the church as the body of Christ, Paul fell to his knees in prayer. The second prayer is recorded at the end of chapter three. I would like to look at the *characteristics* of these two prayers, observing the things that are outward. Then I would like to look at their *content*, noting the inward parts of prayer.

CHARACTERISTICS OF PAUL'S PRAYERS

Motivated by Good News

First of all, we find the *motive* for Paul's prayer. What was it that would cause this apostle to go to prayer? He told us:

Therefore I also, after I heard of your faith in the Lord Jesus and your love for all the saints . . . (Ephesians 1:15 NKJV)

Do you notice what it was that sent him to prayer? It was good news, not bad news. Unfortunately, it seems that the most common circumstances that motivate us to pray are trouble, sickness, distress, or crisis. The story is told that years ago a ship at sea was going down in a storm, and the captain announced over the loudspeaker, "To prayers! To prayers! To prayers!" An elegant, refined woman went up to him and said, "Captain, has it come to this?" In other words, "Is it so desperate now that we are going to have to use prayer as a life preserver?" They hadn't been praying on the days when there was no storm, but when the storm struck and the ship was going down, it was time to start praying. Isn't that the sort of thing that causes many of us to pray today? It is the crisis rather than the time of rejoicing. It is bad news rather than good news that prompts us to prayer.

Now, don't misunderstand me. Should we pray at those times? By all means! But is that the only time we should pray? Shouldn't we have another motive? Shouldn't good news move us to prayer? Paul was saying, in essence, "When I heard about your faith—faith in God, faith in Christ—and then I heard of your love to the brethren, that moved me to prayer." It was good news that prompted him to pray.

Intercessory

Now the second thing to note is that Paul's prayers were *intercessory:*

> [I] *do not cease to give thanks for you, making mention of you in my prayers.* (Ephesians 1:16 NKJV)

You'll find that same thing when you turn to the prayer in the third chapter:

> *That He would grant you, according to the riches of His glory . . .* (Ephesians 3:16 NKJV)

We do not find Paul praying here for himself. Don't misunderstand me—I know he prayed for himself. He told us in 2 Corinthians 12 that he had a thorn in the flesh and that he went to the Lord about it. In fact, he made it a matter of very definite prayer three times because it was of great concern to him. Now that was a personal matter. But you will notice that the recorded prayers of the apostle Paul are all intercessory, praying for others.

Have you ever stopped to think that this is an area in which you can engage? There are many folk today who say, "I'm not able to teach, I'm not able to preach, I'm not called as a missionary, I can't sing in the choir, and I can't do even personal work." My friend, you can pray. Actually, prayer is one of the gifts of the Holy Spirit. One of the greatest ministries that you and I can have today is to follow Paul's example and engage in a ministry of praying for others.

Brief

The third thing to note is the *brevity* of his prayers. Both prayers here in Ephesians are brief. In fact, all the prayers of Scripture are quite brief. The Lord Jesus said in Matthew 6:7 (NKJV), "And when you pray, do not use vain repetitions as the heathen do. For they think that they will be heard for their many words." One of Moses' greatest prayers for Israel is recorded in only four verses (Deuteronomy 9:26–29). Elijah, on top of Mount Carmel as he stood alone for God against the prophets of Baal, prayed a great prayer that is only two verses long (1 Kings 18:36–37). Nehemiah's great prayer is recorded in only seven verses (Nehemiah 1:5–11). The prayer of our Lord in John 17 takes only three minutes to read in the Greek. Martin Luther argued that the fewer the words, the better the prayer. A great many people think that a long prayer means we are being heard or that we are extra pious or that somehow or other we are being very religious. A long prayer is no indication that we are being heard. We may be just repeating ourselves.

We need to recognize the fact that we are taking God's time when we pray. Don't misunderstand—He is willing to listen. But we are very careful about composing a letter that we send to some prominent individual. And if we are going to have an interview with someone important, we turn over in our minds what we are going to say when we get there be-

The little country church was packed out, as they always were for those "protracted meetings," as they used to call them. I said, "Let's pray," and I shut my eyes. Then I heard a tremendous shuffling, but I didn't dare open my eyes because I was a young preacher then, and I didn't want to be irreverent. I kept my eyes closed until I said, "Amen." When I opened them, I didn't see a soul! I thought, *What happened? They all walked out on me while I prayed!* But then they began to come up between the pews just like the corn comes up—a few here, a few there—and in a minute they were all back in their pews again. They had been kneeling on the hard wooden floor!

I think kneeling is a good position. I hope you take that position when you pray privately. Get down on your knees—in fact, get down on your face before God. You see, man today is in rebellion against God. Did you ever notice the language that God used even for His chosen people? He said, "You stiff-necked . . ." (Acts 7:51 NKJV). And all too often the same term could be used for you and me. Stiff-necked!

There are two words for "worship" in the New Testament. One means to bow the head, the other is to bend the knee. You can either genuflect—that is, bow the knee—or you can bend the head. But we are stiff-necked. We want to look up in the face of the Deity. God says, "Get down before Me." The very fact that we bow is a recognition that He is sovereign and that we are to be obedient to Him. My, how this generation needs to learn that we don't treat God as an equal! We are to treat Him as the Lord of heaven, and we do well to go down on our faces before Him.

Paul didn't seem to mind bowing before Him. He said, "I bow my knees before God." We need to learn to get our bodies into a subordinate position.

THE CONTENT OF PAUL'S PRAYERS

Now the *content* of the prayers of Paul is quite interesting also. Let's take a little time to consider the inward parts of prayer.

With Thanksgiving

We find there is a note of *thanksgiving* running through all of Paul's prayers. Thanksgiving should characterize all our prayers. Notice again how Paul wrote to the Ephesian believers:

> [I] *do not cease to give thanks for you, making mention of you in my prayers.* (Ephesians 1:16 NKJV)

You will find thanksgiving in his instructions to the Philippian believers also:

> *Be anxious for nothing, but in everything by prayer and supplication, with thanksgiving, let your requests be made known to God.* (Philippians 4:6 NKJV)

Now "with thanksgiving" is a very strange expression in this context. Paul said that when you bring your requests to

God you also are to come with thanksgiving! There have been several ways of explaining that. Some have said that what Paul really meant was for you to thank God *after* you get your answer. But the interesting thing is that the same tense of the verb is used throughout the passage, thus it cannot be so interpreted. Paul said that at the very moment you make your request you are to thank Him—right then and there. Others have tried to interpret it as meaning that you should thank Him for past favors when you make requests for future favors. The only thing is, Paul didn't say that. Paul said you are to thank Him for the very request you have just made.

Somebody says, "Well, wait a minute. He may not answer." But Paul also said that He *will* answer. I believe one of the worst misnomers Christians use today is "I have unanswered prayer." Have you ever stopped to think what an insult that is to God? What you are really saying is this: "I took a request to God, and He didn't hear me," "He wouldn't listen to me," or "He refused to answer it." May I say to you, if you are a child of God and you brought a request to Him, He has heard and answered your prayer. But somebody says, "Wait a minute! I know that, practically speaking, I have unanswered prayers!" My friend, again may I resist you and say, you do *not* have unanswered prayers! You did get the answer. You simply didn't like it, so you call it an unanswered prayer. May I say to you, God said, "No," and *no* is a good answer. Why don't you accept from God His *no*? Why don't you put the blame where it belongs and say, "I do not have unanswered prayers, but I just don't seem to be praying in the will of God"?

He says *no* many times and, frankly, I'm of the opinion that it is His best answer. When I was growing up, I never took a request to my dad that he did not answer. He *always* answered. But the best answer that he ever gave was *no*. I remember one time I asked my dad for a bicycle, and he said yes. But when I asked for a shotgun, he said no. That was the best answer. Likewise, God always answers with the best possible answer, and we are to make our requests with thanksgiving.

Oh, my friend, Paul always had a note of thanksgiving in his prayers. Part of that thanksgiving came out of his knowledge that God would always hear and answer. When he came to God he would say, "Here is the request," and he would lay it out before Him. Then he'd say, "Lord, thank You for hearing and answering my prayer." He always got an answer. And you, if you are God's child, will get an answer.

Directed to the Father

Now, there is another thing that identifies Paul's prayers. Will you notice this: he prayed *to God the Father*. Somebody says, "You are being technical now. Aren't you splitting hairs?" Yes, but I want to be very frank with you. I think it is very important to pray correctly. Let me illustrate: I went to ask about an important matter when I was in Portland, Oregon. Believe me, I got the runaround! They passed me from one man to another. Finally I said, "I want to talk to the man who *knows*. Don't send me to somebody else. Send me to the man who can make the decision." Then I called for a friend of mine who worked there, he came down from his office, and the whole matter was resolved in about three seconds. It is well to go to the right person. We are technical in situations down here. So what about our prayer life? I think we had better be careful there also.

Paul prayed directly to God the Father. Listen to him:

> *That the God of our Lord Jesus Christ, the Father of glory, may give to you . . .* (Ephesians 1:17 NKJV)

Then over in Ephesians 3:14 (NKJV) he said:

> *For this reason I bow my knees to the Father of our Lord Jesus Christ.*

Paul was being very scriptural, because the Lord Jesus said to His apostles:

> *And in that day you will ask Me nothing. Most assuredly, I say to you, whatever you ask the Father in My name He will give you. Until now you have asked nothing in My name. Ask, and you will receive, that your joy may be full.* (John 16:23–24 NKJV)

To paraphrase what the Lord Jesus Christ said, "Here is a new way of praying. You have never prayed this way before. Don't pray to Me directly. Pray to God the Father in My name."

Remember, when you and I pray to the Son, we lose the benefit of His intercession. He is our great Intercessor. When we pray to God the Father, the Lord Jesus is at God's right hand, and He "lives to make intercession" for us (Hebrews 7:25 NKJV). He says, "That is one of mine down there who is praying. I laid down My life for him. Father, I want You to hear and answer his prayer." We lose the benefit of our Intercessor when we attempt to go directly to the Lord Jesus with our requests.

Now, you say, that is a technicality. Sure it is. Do I think Jesus would hear if we prayed to Him? Of course He would hear. But when I pray, I want the benefit of everything God has to offer. And, my friend, don't we want to be scriptural? He said, "Until now you have asked nothing in My name. Ask, and you will receive, that your joy may be full." I may be splitting hairs, but I am just saying what is here in the Scripture, if you please. "Ask the Father in My name." This is the thing that Jesus emphasized.

Requested Spiritual Understanding

As we consider the content of Paul's prayers, it's important to note that he requested *spiritual understanding*. I do think Paul prayed for material things. We know that he asked for the removal of his "thorn in the flesh," and he prayed for others who were sick. He also prayed that they might have a good journey. So he did pray for material things. But the interesting thing here is that Paul was not praying for physical advantages or material possessions.

You and I are surfeited with secularism in our contemporary society. Today we even measure spiritual enterprises by that which is material, and that is unfortunate. I believe that right now some of the finest works of God are suffering financially. This business today of saying God is blessing a ministry or a church simply because the money is pouring in is totally false—I can name a whole lot of religious rackets that are bringing in the money, my friend. Prosperity is not the measure of success, not before God.

Spiritual understanding was what Paul prayed for, and certainly this is what we need.

> *. . . That Christ may dwell in your hearts through faith; that you, being rooted and grounded in love, may be able to comprehend with all the saints what is the width and length and depth and height—to know the love of Christ which passes knowledge; that you may be filled with all the fullness of God.* (Ephesians 3:17–19 NKJV)

You will find the same thought back in chapter 1:

> *. . . That the God of our Lord Jesus Christ, the Father of glory, may give to you the spirit of wisdom and revelation in the knowledge of Him, the eyes of your understanding being enlightened; that you may know what is the hope of His calling, what are the riches of the glory of His inheritance in the saints.* (Ephesians 1:17–18 NKJV)

Paul was praying here for that which is spiritual, that they might have illumination and understanding and know the love of Christ. How many times do we pray for that? Frankly, that is what I'd like to have. "Oh," you say, "don't you want to pray for health?" Yes. "Don't you want to pray that all obligations be met?" Yes. But after we've done that, what about spiritual understanding? Paul said it passes knowledge. This means your IQ won't help you here. It is something that only the Spirit of God can give you. For:

"Eye has not seen, nor ear heard, nor have entered into the heart of man the things which God has prepared for those who love Him." But God has revealed them to us through His Spirit. For the Spirit searches all things, yes, the deep things of God. (1 Corinthians 2:9–10 NKJV)

The Spirit is the One who leads us and guides us into all truth. We need today to have a fresh anointing of the Spirit of God to understand divine truth.

I am amazed at the error that is creeping into the church today. In fact, I am overwhelmed by it. Heresy is breaking out all over. Why? Because we haven't been praying for that which passes knowledge. We need to be praying for a spiritual understanding of the Word of God, my friend. Never have we needed that as we need it in this hour. I see man after man going off on a tangent. Men who I never dreamed would veer from the truth are today veering from the truth. We need to pray for each other that the "eyes of our understanding" be opened and that we may understand divine truth.

Now it may seem to you that I'm way out in left field when I say that. Perhaps you are saying, "I've been praying for an automobile—next year's models are coming out and I need a new car. Isn't it all right to pray about that?" Sure. But when you pray for that, also ask for a little understanding about how to drive it, as well as a little spiritual knowledge—spiritual knowledge to understand divine truths.

Requested Spiritual Power

That's not all. Paul requested *spiritual power*, and spiritual power is not measured by horses or kilowatts or what is under the hood of a car. Will you listen to him:

> *. . . And what is the exceeding greatness of His power toward us who believe, according to the working of His mighty power . . .* (Ephesians 1:19 NKJV)

He said in essence, "I'm praying that you not only have an understanding but that you have a power, a dynamic, in your life." What is that power? Well, the norm back in the Old Testament was the power of Jehovah "which brought you out of Egypt"; that was always the measuring rod of power. God would say to Israel, "I will do this for you, and I am Jehovah who brought you out of the land of Egypt." That was power. He did it by miracle-working power. But that is not the norm today for believers.

The norm today is this:

. . . Which He worked in Christ when He raised Him from the dead and seated Him at His right hand in the heavenly places. (Ephesians 1:20 NKJV)

That is resurrection power. Paul could say, ". . . That I may know Him and the power of His resurrection" (Philippians 3:10 NKJV). What do you and I know today about resurrection power? What do we know of having that power which worked in Jesus, brought Him up from the dead, and put Him at God's right hand? Think with me for a moment. As long as you and I are in these earthly bodies, we will never get rid of this old nature, but this old nature needs to be put in the place of death in order that we might live by the power of the Holy Spirit working through our new nature. Do we know anything about that power today? Have you felt that power surging through you?

I once rode with a man who was kind enough to take me out to his country club to play golf. He was driving one of those large luxury cars. He said, "You know, McGee, I have to watch the speedometer all the time because of the tremendous power of this car. The other day I was driving up to Portland, and I was going a hundred miles an hour before I knew it—but the police officer knew it! I just put my foot down on the accelerator, and oh, what power!" I said, "I wish that kind of power was in my life." Wouldn't you like to start living by that kind of power? Oh, not under a hood, but that power that raised Jesus from the dead! And that's not all of it. God's power that raised Jesus from the dead also "seated Him at His right hand in the heavenly places."

Power! I'll tell you what is power: Paul said in effect, "I pray that the power, which brought Jesus back from the dead and then took Him off this earth in a glorified body back yonder to God's right hand, might work in you." We need to pray for that, do we not? And honestly, do we know much about that kind of power? Is our praying today really laying hold of God?

I'll tell this corny story, if you don't mind. The first time I went back to John Brown University, a group of students took me on a tour. They asked if I'd like to see the "flying field." (They call them airports today.) I said, "Well, I've been wanting to see a field fly." I went out, and I discovered this: you don't do any flying on a flying field. That's where you take off. Flying is done up yonder.

Suppose you go out to the airport, you get into the plane, you race the motor, you roll down the runway, and then you come back and put it in the hangar. We can say we've been out to the airport and that we made it to the end of the runway, but we never took off! How many times do we really take off in prayer? How many times do we really pray? How many times do we really lay hold of God? I wonder if God says, "Your prayer meetings are like flying fields. You ought to take off, but many of you never do. You just race your motors and go back to the hangar, and you wonder why there is no vitality. You wonder why there is no strength and why there is little interest in prayer today."

Oh, may God teach us to pray, and to pray as the apostle Paul prayed.

Chapter 10

WHEN PRAYER DOES NOT CHANGE THINGS

THE LITTLE EPISTLE TO THE PHILIPPIANS IS, IN my judgment, not only the most practical epistle but also one that's greatly needed in this day in which we live. Although Paul did not write this letter to correct any doctrine or conduct, he touched on all of the great doctrines and practical truths of the Christian life—including prayer. In fact, he asserted that prayer is the secret of power in the Christian life. Notice what he said:

> **Be anxious for nothing, but in everything by prayer and supplication, with thanksgiving, let your requests be made known to God.** (Philippians 4:6 NKJV)

What Paul did was make a contrast between two indefinite pronouns: *nothing* and *everything*. Let me give you my translation, which I call the McGee-icus Ad Absurdum translation. It goes like this: *Worry* about nothing; *pray* about everything. This is a direct commandment. In other words, Paul said that it is wrong and sinful for a Christian to worry. Most of us would have to confess that we've sinned in this area, because we do worry. But we are not to worry. Instead, we are to pray about everything.

Now these two little indefinite pronouns have tremendous significance. The first one, *nothing*, is probably the most exclusive word there is in the English language—it excludes everything. We are not to worry about a single thing. And the reason we are to worry about nothing is because we are to pray about everything. And just as *nothing* excludes all, *everything* includes all. That means we are to talk to the Lord about everything in our lives.

Years ago, a widow went to Dr. G. Campbell Morgan and asked him, "Dr. Morgan, do you think we ought to pray about the little things in our lives?" And Dr. Morgan, in his characteristic British manner, replied, "Madam, can you mention anything in your life that is big to God?" May I say, when we begin to divide the things in our lives as big or little, we are making a false division. All areas of your life and my life just happen to be very small as far as God is concerned. But even what we call little, He wants us to bring to Him. As believers, we need to get in the habit of bringing *everything* to Him in prayer—excluding *nothing*. So these two little pronouns are exact opposites. Nothing means *nothing*, and everything means *everything*.

When Paul said that a Christian is not to worry, he was not advancing a foolish philosophy of shutting our eyes to reality and denying that disease and sickness and death and trouble and pain are realities. Paul was not saying that we are to pray as if those things don't exist. He never indulged in that kind of foolish philosophy at all. He said that the reason we are to worry about nothing is because everything is to be removed from the realm of worry and moved over to the area of prayer.

I'd like to illustrate this with a little joke I heard years ago about a man who couldn't sleep one night. He rolled and tossed, and his wife finally said to him, "What is the matter? Why can't you sleep?" He said, "I owe the tax man six thousand dollars, the note is coming due, and I can't pay it." "Well," his wife said, "you get up, dress, and go over and tell the tax man that you can't pay him. Then come back and go to sleep and let *him* stay awake." May I say to you, my friends, that is exactly what Paul the apostle was really saying here. Paul was saying that when we tell God everything, it becomes *His* problem. We have the right as His children to go to Him in prayer and say, "This is something for *You* to handle" and then turn everything over to Him. Worry about nothing; pray about everything.

I personally do not think there is anything in the Christian's life that should not be made a matter of prayer to God. It doesn't make any difference what it is. He is our heavenly Father, and we can talk to Him very frankly. We can open and unburden our hearts to Him as we can to no one else.

The story is told that when the Panama Canal was under

construction, the families of some of the workers were brought down to visit. One young engineer lived out on a houseboat with his wife and little boy. Every afternoon this young engineer would get into a little rowboat and row out to the houseboat. He would take a great sheaf of blueprints of the Panama Canal with him to work on at home with his family near him.

One evening he had all of his blueprints spread out, and his little boy was playing at his feet with a toy wagon. A wheel came off of the wagon, and the little fellow sat there and worked with it, but he just couldn't get the wheel back on. Finally, he did what little boys do and began to cry. Now do you think the father ignored the little fellow? He might have said, "Son, go on and find your mother. I'm working on the great Panama Canal, and I can't have you bothering me." But he didn't do that. He put aside the blueprints, sat down on the floor, took up the little fellow, and asked him what was the matter. The little boy held up the wagon in one hand and a wheel in the other. And what to the little boy was a major project, to the father was practically nothing. With just a twist of the wrist, he put the wheel on. Then he kissed his son's tears away, patted him, put him down on the floor, and the little fellow began playing again.

Now, my friend, it is God who put that father instinct deep down in the human heart of man, because He too is a compassionate Father. When a wheel comes off your wagon, it may look like an impossible problem to you, but

He will hear and answer your cry. If He says no, it is because that is the best answer you could have. After I lost my human father, I lived several years before I turned to God and found that I had a heavenly Father. I learned that I could go to Him with my requests, and He would answer me just as my human father used to do. And, also like my earthly father, many times God's answers are no.

When I was a young pastor in Texas, I went to a certain city to candidate in a church. It was considered to be an outstanding, strategic church. After I'd preached twice that Sunday, I was given a call by the church. Then later they had to come back and tell me that the denomination would not permit them to call me. As I said, it was a strategic church, and they needed a politician, which I was not. But I felt that the Lord had made a great mistake by not letting me go to that church as pastor. Many years later, my wife and I went by that church just to see it. It had gone into liberalism. I said to her, "Do you remember years ago when I thought I should have had the call for that church? I thank God that He heard and answered my prayer the *right* way—not the way I prayed it."

My friend, my heavenly Father had answered my prayer, and I am ashamed of the fact that I did not thank Him at the time. My advice to you is this: instead of saying that God has not answered your prayers, say, "My heavenly Father heard my prayer, but He told me no, which was the right answer." We are to let our requests be made known to God with thanksgiving—knowing that, regardless of how He answers, it will always be the best thing for us.

Notice what Paul said next:

And the peace of God, which surpasses all understanding, will guard your hearts and minds through Christ Jesus. (Philippians 4:7 NKJV)

Scripture speaks of many kinds of peace. There is world peace. We have the assurance that someday peace will cover the earth as the waters cover the sea. It will come through the person of Christ, the Prince of Peace. Also there is the peace that comes when sins are forgiven: "Therefore, having been justified by faith, we have peace with God through our Lord Jesus Christ" (Romans 5:1 NKJV). Then there is the peace that is tranquility. The Lord Jesus said, "Peace I leave with you, My peace I give to you" (John 14:27 NKJV). That is a marvelous peace.

But none of these is the peace mentioned here. This is a peace that cannot be described. In fact, if we could describe it then it wouldn't be the peace mentioned here because Paul said it "surpasses all understanding." I'm of the opinion that this is a peace that a great many of us have experienced. I think it is a peace that sweeps over our souls amidst the troubles and trials of life. It is this peace that gives us confidence that, irrespective of the circumstances, things are going to be worked out for our own good and His glory.

This same peace enables us to face life full on, stand on the wide deck of life and know that it does not make any difference how hard the winds might blow or how high the waves might roll. For this peace "will guard [our] hearts and minds through Christ Jesus." "Guard" is a good word to use. This peace of God will be on guard duty like a sentinel about our hearts and minds. It will protect and keep us through the trials of life.

Now I want you to notice something that has happened. We entered this passage with anxiety and worry. We come out of the passage in peace. Between the two is prayer. Have things changed? No. The problem is still there. The storm may still be raging, the waves still rolling high, the thunder still resounding. Nothing has changed outside, but the one who is praying has changed. Something has happened to the soul, moving the individual from a place of worry to a place where the peace of God now controls the heart and life.

I'm convinced that the primary purpose of prayer is not to change *things* but to change *us*. Our problem today is that we think prayer is a faucet we can turn on to get out of it anything we want. Or it is a mystical hocus-pocus that makes our problems disappear. That's not prayer! Prayer is when we go before our heavenly Father, tell Him everything, and then let Him take over. Once we take our hands off, He begins to move—not necessarily on the things outside, but in our own hearts and lives. Sometimes He puts the wheel back on the wagon and makes it better. But sometimes He doesn't. The thing He's concerned about is changing our hearts.

Oh, how we need to enter into the treasures of real prayer today! Real prayer changes our hearts and lives and brings our thinking, our wills, our plans, and our purposes into conformity with the will of God. How important that is!

Most of us today stand on the fringe of prayer. We've never really entered in. We've never come as a child with absolute simplicity and absolute faith to a Father, knowing that He is going to hear and answer in the best way possible. We need to say to Him, "Lord, we believe but help our unbelief. Help us to enjoy that wonderful intimacy, that glorious privilege, of talking to an omnipotent, omniscient Father who knows what is best for us."

Chapter 11

THE *REAL*
LORD'S PRAYER

THE SEVENTEENTH CHAPTER OF THE GOSPEL OF John is one of the most remarkable chapters in the Bible. It records the longest prayer in Scripture, although it takes only about three minutes to read. (I think that is a good indication of the length of public prayers: if you can't say all you've got to say in three minutes, then you've got too much to say.) The Upper Room Discourse is like climbing a mountain, and this prayer is the pinnacle. It is a great portion of Scripture, and I feel wholly and totally inadequate to deal with it. For this prayer reveals to us a bit of the communication that, I think, passes constantly between the Lord Jesus and the Father in heaven.

Our Lord's entire life was a life of prayer. He often went up into a mountain to pray and even spent entire nights in prayer. In fact, He began His ministry by going into a solitary place to pray. What did He pray for at these times, and what does He continue to pray for now? Well, He prays for you and for me; He is our great Intercessor. And God always hears and answers Jesus' prayer just the way He prays it. God answers my prayer also, but not always the way I pray it— sometimes He must answer my prayer with a no, or He may accomplish what I ask by a completely different method or at a different time. However, Jesus said:

Father, I thank You that You have heard Me. And I know that You always hear Me, but because of the people who are standing by I said this, that they may believe that You sent Me. (John 11:41–42 NKJV)

Although we refer to the prayer beginning, "Our Father in heaven, hallowed be Your name" as "the Lord's Prayer," it is not. That prayer that He gave in the Sermon on the Mount is not the Lord's Prayer, but it is a prayer that He taught to the disciples. When Jesus began with "Our Father," He meant that to be for all the believers. Because when Jesus called God "Father," He meant it in a different sense. After His resurrection, He said to Mary:

I have not yet ascended to My Father; but go to My brethren and say to them, "I am ascending to My Father and your Father, and to My God and your God." (John 20:17 NKJV)

In other words, "I have not yet ascended to *your* Father (yours by the new birth) and to My Father (Mine because of

My position in the Trinity)." Also, Jesus could never have prayed for Himself, "Forgive us our debts, our sins." He never had any sins. So He could not pray that prayer. By the same token, you and I can never pray this prayer of John 17. This is *His* prayer; it is the real Lord's Prayer, for it is the prayer that He Himself prayed directly to the Father.

JESUS PRAYED FOR HIMSELF

I want you to notice that it is neither out of line nor even a mark of selfishness to pray for oneself. I believe that when you and I go to God in prayer, we need to get our own hearts and lives right with God. We need to get in tune with heaven, as it were; every instrument should be tuned up before it is played. So before you and I begin to pray for others, we need to pray for ourselves. That is not selfishness; it is essential.

The preceding four chapters of the Gospel of John (13–16) record what our Lord said to His disciples. Then He stopped speaking to the disciples, and He spoke to the Father for the benefit of His disciples—and for our benefit also. As I've said, He is our great Intercessor, and He is praying today on our behalf.

Now notice how He began His prayer:

> *Jesus spoke these words, lifted up His eyes to heaven, and said: "Father, the hour has come. Glorify Your Son, that Your Son also may glorify You."* (John 17:1 NKJV)

What hour had come? Remember that when He began His ministry at the wedding of Cana, His mother said to Him, "They have no wine." His answer to her was, "Woman, what does your concern have to do with Me? My hour has not yet come" (John 2:3–4 NKJV). Now the hour had come, the hour when He would pay for your sins and mine. As He spoke, the clock was striking the hour that was set way back in eternity, because He was "the Lamb slain from the foundation of the world" (Revelation 13:8 NKJV). It was the hour when all of creation would see the love of God displayed as He took your sins and my sins upon Himself and died a vicarious, substitutionary, redemptive death for us and then completed the transaction by being raised from the dead.

He also said, "Glorify Your Son, that Your Son also may glorify You." The death of Christ demonstrates that God is not the brutal bully in the Old Testament that liberal theologians talk about, but that He is a Father who so loves the world that He would give His only begotten Son (see John 3:16). Then the Son was raised from the dead, ascended back into heaven, and was given a name that is above every name, so that today every knee should bow to Him. Oh, the wealth of meaning that is in this statement of our Lord!

Then He made a startling revelation:

You have given Him authority over all flesh, that He should give eternal life to as many as You have given Him. (John 17:2 NKJV)

He has power over all flesh! He could make this universe and every individual in it bow to Him. He could bring us all into subjection to Him and make robots out of all of us. Although He has the power over all flesh, the last thing He wants to do is wield it in such a way.

You see, the church is God's love gift to Jesus Christ. So He gives "eternal life to as many as [God has] given Him." This brings up the question of election and free will, and I don't want to go into that extensively. There are extremists on both sides of the issue, and the truth is probably somewhere between the two. If God would somehow reveal to me who are the elect ones, I would give the gospel only to them. But God does not do this. He has said that whosoever will may come.

> **And this is eternal life, that they may know You, the only true God, and Jesus Christ whom You have sent.** (John 17:3 NKJV)

That is a legitimate offer to every person. You have no excuse at all if you will not come to Him. It will be your condemnation if you turn down the offer God has made to you.

Does election shut out certain people? No. Life eternal is to know the only true God and Jesus Christ whom He has sent. Do you have a desire to know the true God and Jesus Christ? Then you are not shut out; you must be one of the elect. He gives eternal life to those who have heard the call and have responded down in their hearts. They have come to Christ of their own free will.

"That they may know You" refers not to the amount of knowledge you have, but to the kind of knowledge it is. It is *whom* you know that is all-important. Do you know Jesus Christ? In the same way, it is not the amount of faith you have but the kind of faith that is important. There is an old song called "Only Believe." But only believe what? Only believe in the only One—the Lord Jesus Christ. One can believe in the wrong thing. Therefore, it is the *object* of faith that is so important. Now faith comes by hearing the Word of God. What does the Word of God say? "And this is eternal life, that they may know *You*, the only true God, and Jesus Christ whom You have sent." The gospel is that Jesus died for our sins, was buried, and rose again. Those are the facts. Our knowledge of the facts and our response to that knowledge is faith, and faith is trusting Christ as our own Savior.

Life eternal is to *know* God and to *know* Jesus Christ. Jesus is His name as Savior, and Christ is His title—the Messiah, the King of Israel. To know Him means to grow in grace and in the knowledge of Christ. When we move on in the knowledge of the Lord Jesus Christ, we come to the place of assurance. Anyone without the assurance of salvation is either unsaved or is just a babe in Christ. Such a person needs to move on to the place where he *knows* that he is saved. Many people stay on the fringe of things and are never sure they are saved. This is the reason why the study of the Word of God is so important.

*I have glorified You on the earth. I have finished the
work which You have given Me to do.* (John 17:4 NKJV)

Here the Lord Jesus was handing in His final report to
the Father. He hadn't died on the cross yet; but future tense
for God is just as accurate as past tense. Our Lord Jesus was
going to the cross to die and then would rise again. On the
cross, He said, "It is finished!" (John 19:30 NKJV). That
means our redemption was finished. He had done everything that was necessary. We can put a period there, because
we cannot add a thing to His finished work. Therefore, the
gospel of salvation is not what God is asking you to do, but
what God is telling you that He has already done for you.
Your response to that knowledge is what determines your
salvation.

Our Lord's prayer continued:

*And now, O Father, glorify Me together with Yourself,
with the glory which I had with You before the world
was.* (John 17:5 NKJV)

In Philippians 2, it speaks of Jesus emptying Himself. Some
try to teach that He emptied Himself of His deity. But John
made it very clear that the Word became flesh and that little baby in Mary's lap was God and could have spoken this
universe out of existence. He wasn't just 99.9 percent God;
He was, and is today, 100 percent God. So then what did He
empty Himself of? He emptied Himself of His prerogatives

of deity; He laid aside His glory that He had with God "before the world was."

At Christmastime we make a great deal of the shepherds and the angels and the wise men who came to see Him. Friend, that is not the way it should have been. He is the Lord of glory, and every human being on the face of the earth should have been there to worship Him at the time of His birth. After all, people will travel from all parts of a country—and even all parts of the world—for the funeral of a great political leader. The whole world should have been at the birth of the Lord of glory when He came to earth. Although He could have claimed such homage, instead He laid aside His glory. As He prayed this prayer, He was ready to return to heaven, back to the glory.

JESUS PRAYED FOR HIS DISCIPLES

I have manifested Your name to the men whom You have given Me out of the world. They were Yours, You gave them to Me, and they have kept Your word. (John 17:6 NKJV)

Notice this: "to as many as You have given Him" (verse 2); "to the men whom You have given Me . . . You gave them to Me" (verse 6); "for those whom You have given Me" (verse 9); "those whom You have given Me" (verse 11); and "those whom You gave Me" (verse 12). We are back to the great doctrine of election. And here Jesus talked to the

Father about it. It was a private conversation, but He wanted the disciples to hear it and to know about it. I don't know as much about election as maybe I should. I've read several commentaries on the subject, and the authors don't seem to know much more about it. The reason we know so little about election is because it is God's side, and there are a lot of things that God knows that we don't.

It is a wonderful thing to be able to listen to this prayer and to know that Jesus is at God's right hand talking to the Father about us. If you are one of His, the Lord Jesus has talked to the Father about you today. There is a mystical relationship between the Lord Jesus and His own: they belong to the Father and were given to Jesus Christ. I can't fathom its meaning, but what a wonderful relationship it is!

Now they have known that all things which You have given Me are from You. For I have given to them the words which You have given Me; and they have received them, and have known surely that I came forth from You; and they have believed that You sent Me. (John 17:7–8 NKJV)

Our Lord had given them the words of the Father. That is important. He had not given them property or money or an automobile, but the words of the Father. Jesus testified here that these disciples believed that He came from the Father; they knew who He was. They did not understand His purpose—and certainly not His death and resurrection—but they had made tremendous advances during the three years they had been with Him. They knew He had come from God, and they believed that God had sent Him.

> *I pray for them. I do not pray for the world but for those whom You have given Me, for they are Yours.* (John 17:9 NKJV)

I will make a startling statement, but one that is no more startling than what He made: Jesus Christ does not pray for the world today. His ministry of intercession is for His own who are *in* the world, but He doesn't pray for the world. He *died* for the world; what more could He do?

Next He prayed for two very wonderful things:

> *And all Mine are Yours, and Yours are Mine, and I am glorified in them. Now I am no longer in the world, but these are in the world, and I come to You. Holy Father, keep through Your name those whom You have given Me, that they may be one as We are.* (John 17:10–11 NKJV)

First, He prayed for us to be kept. And we are kept because we have been sealed by the Holy Spirit and because our Savior is praying for us.

His second request was that we should be one. There has been much wrong teaching about this. He prayed for the unity of believers, but He was not talking about an ecumenical movement or asking that we would all join the same denomination. He prayed to the Father that His own might be one. Notice that He wasn't praying to us or to some church authority—He was praying to the Father. And He prayed that we should be one "as We are"—that is, as the Father and the Son are one.

The Father answers every prayer of His Son, and He has answered this one. The Holy Spirit takes all true believers and baptizes them, thereby identifying and unifying them into the body of Christ. The disgrace of it all is that down here the believers are pretty well divided. But there is only one true church, and every believer in Jesus Christ is a member of that church. It is called the body of Christ.

While I was with them in the world, I kept them in Your name. Those whom You gave Me I have kept; and none of them is lost except the son of perdition [Judas Iscariot], *that the Scripture might be fulfilled.* (John 17:12 NKJV)

Here we have election mentioned again, for He said, "Those whom You gave Me . . ." There are certain things that I believe, which to me are not contradictory—but they certainly are paradoxical. The issue of election and free will happens to be one of those. I wish you could have met me when I graduated from seminary. I was a smart boy then, and I thought I had the answer to election and free will. But I have a little more sense now than I had then, and I realize that we simply do not understand it.

But His next statement was very straightforward and easy to understand:

> *But now I come to You, and these things I speak in the*
> *world, that they may have My joy fulfilled in themselves.*
> (John 17:13 NKJV)

Friend, God does not want us to be long-faced, solemn Christians. He came that our lives might be filled with His joy. We need to be reminded of that sometimes, and isn't it nice to know that our Lord is praying about that on our behalf?

Then He went on to say:

> *I have given them Your word; and the world has hated*
> *them because they are not of the world, just as I am not*
> *of the world.* (John 17:14 NKJV)

The Word of God causes problems in the world today. The Bible is the most revolutionary Book there has ever been. It is revolutionary to teach that you cannot save yourself, but that only Christ can save you. And you can't make this world better; only Jesus Christ can do that. That's revolutionary, and the world doesn't want to hear it. They'd rather plant a few flowers and try to clean up pollution. The problem is that the pollution is in the human heart.

We cry and whimper because things are hard down here. The Lord even acknowledged that our lives on this earth would be hard: "In the world you will have tribulation; but be of good cheer, I have overcome the world" (John 16:33 NKJV). We long for the Rapture, imagining that it will be wonderful and that it will bring glory to God—and it will. But let's understand one thing: God gets glory by keeping you and me in the world. So Jesus prayed not that we should be taken out of the world, but that we should be kept from the evil one, Satan:

I do not pray that You should take them out of the world, but that You should keep them from the evil one. (John 17:15 NKJV)

I wouldn't want to be here for a minute if my Lord weren't keeping me from the evil one. But the Lord Jesus has prayed to keep us in the world and to protect us from Satan. If we could learn that, it would enable us to endure more easily our problems and tensions and difficulties and temptations.

He continued:

They are not of the world, just as I am not of the world. Sanctify them by Your truth. Your word is truth. (John 17:16–17 NKJV)

The more we as believers realize this, the more completely we fulfill His will and accomplish His purpose. For the believer is not of the world but is set apart. That's what is meant by "sanctify"—to set apart. And what sets the believer apart is the Word of God. That is, the Word reveals the mind of God; and as we read and study His Word, we are led to set ourselves apart for a particular ministry. So we can serve Him in this world only as we know His Word and are obedient to it.

Our Lord made it clear that we do have a purpose in this world: to bear witness of Him.

As You sent Me into the world, I also have sent them into the world. And for their sakes I sanctify Myself, that they also may be sanctified by the truth. (John 17:18–19 NKJV)

He set Himself apart to be identified with us, and likewise we ought to be identified with Him in this world.

JESUS PRAYED FOR ALL BELIEVERS

I do not pray for these alone, but also for those who will believe in Me through their word. (John 17:20 NKJV)

He had you and me in mind when He prayed this prayer! How marvelous! Now, many centuries later, we can know that our great High Priest is still praying for us. And what is He praying? That is revealed in the next verse:

That they all may be one, as You, Father, are in Me, and I in You; that they also may be one in Us, that the world may believe that You sent Me. (John 17:21 NKJV)

This prayer has been answered, for believers are one in Christ and the church is one body. The minute any sinner trusts Christ, that sinner is put into the body of Christ. If believers would manifest that union to others, the world would be more impressed with Christ today. Too often the world sees believers hating each other, which may be one of the reasons why they will not accept Christ.

Then He said something that is really quite wonderful:

> *And the glory which You gave Me I have given them, that they may be one just as We are one: I in them, and You in Me; that they may be made perfect in one, and that the world may know that You have sent Me, and have loved them as You have loved Me.* (John 17:22–23 NKJV)

"I in them, and You in Me." Only the Spirit of God can accomplish that. The unity that exists between the Father and the Son is the unity that is to exist between the believer and the Lord Jesus Christ! "And have loved them as You have loved Me" means that God loves *you* as much as He loves the Lord Jesus Christ. That boggles the mind!

God created man with a free will; and, even though man sinned, God wants his fellowship. There are other creatures on the earth, but man is the only creature with whom God can have fellowship.

> *Father, I desire that they also whom You gave Me may be with Me where I am, that they may behold My glory*

which You have given Me; for You loved Me before the foundation of the world. (John 17:24 NKJV)

It will be heaven to be with Him in perfect fellowship. I take it that this was God's purpose in creating man. Heaven is going to be wonderful, and it will be important that every one of His sheep is there with Him. Each one will have a contribution to make.

He also mentioned His glory, and to behold the glory of the Lord Jesus will be the satisfaction of the believer. Moses asked to see the glory of God (see Exodus 33:18), and Philip asked to see the Father (see John 14:8). Sometimes we get a glimpse of nature's glory in a rainbow or a sunset. Think what it will be like when we come into His presence and behold His glory! That is the goal to which we are moving.

But first we must know Him and acknowledge who He is and what He has done for us. His prayer continued:

O righteous Father! The world has not known You, but I have known You; and these have known that You sent Me. (John 17:25 NKJV)

Being sent from the Father actually embraced His entire mission of redemption. Anyone who is a believer knows that the Father sent Him, and the purpose was for Him to die for our sins.

The last thing He mentioned in His prayer was that His love might be in our hearts and lives:

And I have declared to them Your name, and will declare it, that the love with which You loved Me may be in them, and I in them. (John 17:26 NKJV)

We talk so much about grace and about faith, and rightly so. Yet the great desire of His heart is that His love should be manifested in the lives of those whom He has redeemed. That should put us down on our faces before Him. My friend, how much of His love is manifested in you?

The Lord Jesus Christ is our great High Priest. This is the great truth of the Epistle to the Hebrews. In the Old Testament economy, the high priest wore an ephod of beauty and glory, which was joined on each shoulder by two onyx stones with the names of the tribes of Israel engraved on them. Thus he carried the names of the children of Israel with him on his shoulders when he went into the presence of God. This speaks of the strength and power of our own High Priest, Jesus Christ, who "is also able to save to the uttermost those who come to God through Him, since He always lives to make intercession for them" (Hebrews 7:25 NKJV). Christ is *able* to save us, you see. He has strength and power.

Also on the breastplate of the high priest were twelve precious stones, arranged three in a row in four rows across his breast. On each was the name of a tribe of Israel. When the high priest went into God's presence wearing the breastplate, he pictured the Lord Jesus Christ who is at the right hand of God interceding for us. Likewise, the Lord not only carries us on His shoulders—the place of strength and power—but He also carries us on His breast, on His heart, which speaks of His love. The God of the universe, who has all glory and power, loves us and is taking us to His Father in prayer!

PART II

Let Us Pray:

A STUDY OF "THE LORD'S PRAYER"

INTRODUCTION TO
LET US PRAY

ANYONE WHO SPEAKS OR WRITES ON THE so-called Lord's Prayer has entered a field of controversy because of the two extreme interpretations of the prayer—the ultraliberal and the superconservative. Any exposition on this prayer comes into the range of the heavy artillery of one or both of these groups. My purpose in examining it is not to enter the field of apologetics or logistics, but to strengthen the deep desire for reality in prayer in these days of superficiality.

The only excuse for studying the prayer is to lay upon the heart of God's people the urgency for knocking on His door, the necessity for asking, and the importunity for seeking. Nevertheless, in our zeal and enthusiasm we have stressed the importance of knocking at the right door, asking in the proper way, and seeking in the correct direction.

This message is sent out with the prayer that it may stimulate God's people to "pray without ceasing" (1 Thessalonians 5:17 NKJV).

Chapter 12

IS THE LORD'S
PRAYER FOR TODAY?

IN THE THINKING OF MANY THROUGH THE YEARS and into the present hour, the following glorious petitions fall under the caption of "the Lord's Prayer":

> *Our Father in heaven, hallowed be Your name. Your kingdom come. Your will be done on earth as it is in heaven. Give us this day our daily bread. And forgive us our debts, as we forgive our debtors. And do not lead us into temptation, but deliver us from the evil one. For Yours is the kingdom and the power and the glory forever. Amen.* (Matthew 6:9–13 NKJV)

But should this really be called "the Lord's Prayer"? The confusion in title is well illustrated by a conversation between two men who were boasting of their respective knowledge of the Bible. The first man commented to his friend, "Why, you do not even know the Lord's Prayer." The friend stated that he certainly did and began to pray, "Now I lay me down to sleep. I pray the Lord my soul to keep. If I should die before I wake, I pray the Lord my soul to take." When he had concluded, the challenger said, "Well, you sure fooled me. I didn't think you knew it."

For the want of accurate information, much the same confusion surrounds our use of the title "the Lord's Prayer." Technically speaking, John 17 is our Lord's prayer—that is the prayer He prayed. He could never have prayed the prayer recorded in Matthew 6 and Luke 11 that, to us, has always been known as "the Lord's Prayer."

There are many instances that show clearly that this could not have been our Lord's own prayer. For instance, He could not have used the first word *our*. Have you taken note of the fact that His relationship with God is different from that which we hold? We call Him "Father" because of regeneration; He called Him "Father" because of His place in the Godhead. He was always careful to use the terms "My Father" and "your Father," never "*our* Father." Also, Luke recorded, "Forgive us our sins" (Luke 11:4 NKJV). The Lord Jesus had no sins to confess. As far as we know, He never took an offering into the temple for Himself—He was the sinless One who was able to ask, "Which of you convicts Me of sin?" (John 8:46 NKJV).

Therefore, strictly speaking, this is "the Disciples' Prayer." But with this differentiation drawn, and for the sake of ease of writing, we shall use the accustomed title, "the Lord's Prayer."

Now the charge is often made against those of us who are conservative and premillennial that we slight the Lord's Prayer, do not reverence it, and that we ignore it altogether. A further charge is made that we strike it out of our Bibles and consequently never use it in our public services at all. This charge is obviously untrue. I believe that the Lord's Prayer has a real message for us, and I trust that studying it will give us a new appreciation and reverence for this prayer.

I have a notion that the Lord's Prayer is used many times and in many places today simply because it is something with which to begin a service. Those with elaborate rituals and extended liturgy always include this prayer. It has been used by the most unlikely groups at the most inopportune times. For instance, it is a matter of record that at the 1893 World's Fair in Chicago a strange thing occurred at the opening of the World's Congress of Religion. There were present Buddhists, Hindus, Taoists, in fact, representatives of all religions of the world. And they all stood and in unison repeated the Lord's Prayer!

Let us consider the mechanics of this prayer. It was given as a model to the disciples in response to their request for Jesus to teach them how to pray. Every born-again child of God has a longing to have fellowship with God. Beloved, it is the mark of a regenerated person that, having come to the knowledge of God, he prays! You may remember that when Ananias of Damascus was sent over to see Saul of Tarsus he was told, "You'll know him—for behold, he is praying" (see Acts 9:11).

There are two characteristics that stand out in the Lord's Prayer. May I mention them, for they are so important. First of all there is the simplicity of it, and then its brevity. Simplicity and brevity ought always to characterize genuine prayer.

Looking more closely into its structure, we find that there are also two major divisions in this prayer. There is that part of it that deals with the glory of God: "Your kingdom come. Your will be done on earth as it is in heaven." And then there is that other division that deals with the wants of men: "Give us this day our daily bread." We will look closer at these petitions in a later chapter.

Now although it was given by our Lord as a model of prayer, this prayer is never repeated in the Book of Acts. As far as we know, the apostolic church never used the Lord's Prayer. As a matter of rich spiritual exercise you will find it profitable to compare this prayer to Paul's prayers in the Epistle to the Ephesians. I think you will find that Paul moved to a higher spiritual realm in his praying.

There is something else that we need to note: the Lord's Prayer is included in the Sermon on the Mount. Every person who comes to the Sermon on the Mount ought to do so in a very thoughtful manner, for here we have two extreme positions today. There are those (usually liberals) who say, "The Sermon on the Mount is all the religion I need." A graduate of a seminary in New York City once told me, "All I need today is the Sermon on the Mount. You can take the rest of the Bible and destroy it so far as I am concerned."

Unfortunately, there are a great many people who feel that way. Then there is another group that feels this prayer has no meaning for us today and may as well be taken out of the Bible.

This whole difficulty has arisen largely because of a misunderstanding of the *interpretation* versus the *application* of Scripture—two vastly different things between which we must draw a sharp distinction. The Sermon on the Mount may not have an interpretation for us, but we can find great riches in its application.

To make clear this point, let us turn to the Book of Joshua where we read, "Arise, go over this Jordan" (Joshua 1:2 NKJV). Now, how many of us have ever been over the Jordan River? If you have not, you certainly have failed to keep that part of Scripture, for it very clearly states—and there is no misunderstanding so literal a statement—"Arise, go over this Jordan." But you and I understand that this was written for another people and another day. So we understand that it has an interpretation specifically for Joshua and the children of Israel relative to crossing the Jordan River into the promised land.

But, beloved, it also has a very wonderful application for us. We can take it today as a commandment for our own heart and soul. We are to understand that the River Jordan is a picture of the death, burial, and resurrection of Jesus Christ. He wants us as believers to leave the wilderness and its manna and cross over onto resurrection ground. For "if then you were raised with Christ, seek those things which

163

are above, where Christ is, sitting at the right hand of God" (Colossians 3:1 NKJV). We are to cross over the Jordan into the promised land—the place of blessing.

So, you see, there was an interpretation for the children of Israel, but there is an application for all believers. When there is an interpretation that is not directly for you and me, there is always an application that extends to us.

Now the Sermon on the Mount was given to people who were under the Law; they were certainly not under grace. It was a manifesto of the King; it was the law of the kingdom. But the church, which is under grace, will be the bride of Christ—she will reign with Him someday, and it has been the custom of a queen never to despise the law of the kingdom. The queen must still measure up to the laws of the kingdom.

Today, there are too many people declaring themselves as conservative in their theology, and therefore a part of the body of Christ, who live lives that despise the ethics of the Sermon on the Mount, the law of the kingdom. What a sad commentary it is on the cause we represent! If those same people would go to the top of the mountain, the scene of the Sermon on the Mount, and listen to the King, they could not look lightly upon sin. When an elderly gentleman who could not hear well was asked a question as to his ethics, not quite understanding, he replied, "I have traded my Essex for a Hudson." And I fear that many today have traded in their ethics for something else. We have such low standards, and we need desperately to get back to some good, old-fashioned virtues of common honesty and integrity. If you and I are to reign with Him, dare we despise these things?

When we stand in the revealing light of the Sermon on the Mount, how great is the need to reverence it. It is not a cover for sin—it condemns us. It is not a savior, for there is no mention of salvation, faith, or grace. It is a judge that looks at us as sinners and causes us to flee to the Savior for refuge. Law is justice, not mercy. When, in sorrow, I consider where I stand under the justice of that law, I can turn with rejoicing to the mercy of His grace, for it is "not by works of righteousness which we have done, but according to His mercy He saved us" (Titus 3:5 NKJV).

Let us not despise the law of our King that shall one day prevail on this earth; rather, let us look at the gem nestled in the very heart of this great Sermon on the Mount. Seen in its proper perspective, the Lord's Prayer will have a new meaning for you. It is a guide to prayer; we ought to reverence it and we ought to stand in awe and wonder before it. We dare not repeat it carelessly in a church service, for the time may appear when the praying of it will become the cry of our hearts.

But our question is, is the Lord's Prayer for today? I think the key to the answer is in the Gospel of Luke. There he wrote that the disciples went to the Lord Jesus and said, "Teach us to pray" (see Luke 11:1). So He gave them this model prayer. Then He gave them a parable that, in my judgment, holds the placement of the Lord's Prayer for us in this day. It is the parable about the man who, having unexpected guests arrive during the night, knocked on the door of his neighbor and asked that he loan him a loaf of bread to feed his guests. The neighbor replied that the family was asleep and he did not wish to have the household disturbed, so the man would have to wait until the morning. But the man continued knocking until the neighbor got out of bed and let him have the bread, not because of feelings of friendship but because of the importunity of the person knocking. (See Luke 11:5–8.)

In taking this parable as the key, we must remember that Luke gave us parables by contrast. The point, simply stated, is this: do you think God slumbers? He does not: "Behold, He who keeps Israel shall neither slumber nor sleep" (Psalm 121:4 NKJV). Do you feel that you have to bang on the door to get Him to hear you? He is ready to hear and answer the prayers of those who come to Him. But He also says that, like this man, you are to go persistently and knock on the door:

> *So I say to you, ask, and it will be given to you; seek, and you will find; knock, and it will be opened to you.* (Luke 11:9 NKJV)

If you can pray the Lord's Prayer as that man, standing at the door of his neighbor at midnight—knocking to gain something in the time of emergency—then I say to you, use the Lord's Prayer. But do not make it a vain repetition. It was given to avoid vain repetition. When it becomes the cry of the human heart, then that person can say, "Our Father in heaven, hallowed be Your name. Your kingdom come. Your will be done on earth as it is in heaven," knowing that God does not slumber and that He wants to hear and answer prayer. Have you prayed like that to God recently? Have you gone to Him persistently, knocking at midnight?

Ask . . . seek . . . knock, and it will be opened to you!

Chapter 13

ON SPEAKING
TERMS WITH GOD

MEN, GREAT IN BOTH SCHOLARSHIP AND HUMBLE faith, have sat before the Lord's Prayer intent upon finding the underlying richness of its perfection. Resultant of their research and study, some have determined that the Lord's Prayer falls into six petitions; others have felt that there are eight; while the opinions of the great Augustine and Martin Luther were agreed that there are seven petitions. This point we will not here debate. However, I am of the thinking that there are three petitions relating to God and identified by the little pronoun *Your*—"Hallowed be Your name," "Your kingdom come," and "Your will be done." And then there are four petitions relating to man and marked out by the words *our* and *us*—"Give us this day our daily bread," "Forgive us our debts," "Do not lead us into temptation," and "Deliver us from the evil one."

Although the above "breaking down" of the Lord's Prayer is essential to our understanding, we will turn from it and concern ourselves, for the present, with the introduction or invocation of the prayer. Three striking statements lie here in the introduction: "Our Father," "in heaven," and "hallowed be Your name."

OUR FATHER...

As we go into the study, we come first of all to the statement "Our Father." This was startling to the Old Testament saint, for as far as we know he never, under any conditions, called God "Father" in a personal way. It is true that Israel, as a nation, was called a "son." God commanded Moses to tell Pharaoh that Israel was His son and to let him go (see Exodus 4:22–23). But you do not find individual Israelites calling God "Father." He was the Father of the nation, of His people, but the individual was the son of Abraham, Isaac, and Jacob. So they did not approach God as a father.

Now let us note carefully that Moses was called a "servant" (Exodus 14:31 NKJV); following the thread, we see that David also was called a "servant" (2 Samuel 7:5 NKJV); and still following the development of relationship, we come to the Ethiopian eunuch and find that he becomes a "son" of God (see Acts 8:36–38 and John 1:12). How? Through faith in Jesus Christ! You can see something radical has taken place!

Now, in a very real sense, all of mankind are the sons of God by creation. Paul, when speaking to the Athenians on Mars Hill, said, "For we are also His offspring" (Acts 17:28

NKJV). But the word he used is not that of sonship—*huios* in the Greek—rather, *genos*, which carries the meaning that we are His creation. God created Adam, who was called a "son of God." Then Adam sinned, and after the Fall he begat a son who was like him in his fallen nature. From then on, mankind was no longer considered sons of God in any personal way whatsoever.

I want to say this kindly, but one of the most pernicious lies in our land is that of the universal fatherhood of God and the universal brotherhood of man. There has never been spawned in the depths of hell a thing more deceiving. A great scholar of the past called them "a moronic simplification." Reduced to simple English, anyone who speaks of the universal fatherhood of God and the universal brotherhood of man speaks as a moron.

I am confident that the Word of God provides sharp proof of the fallacy of this teaching. Not too many years ago there was a case in Ohio of a one-year-old boy being kidnapped from his parents. Five years later a little lad was located in an orphanage who looked as they felt their son would look at that age. They concluded that their long quest was ended and ordered a blood test to determine if the boy was their long-lost child. But, sadly, he was not, and the newspapers carried the headline: "Science Shatters Dream." Likewise, Scripture shatters the dream of those who long to establish the teaching of the universal fatherhood of God and the universal brotherhood of man. There is a blood test that must be made, and we are declared to be sons of God only through this blood test! We are sons of God only through a washing by the blood of Christ. It is that blood that establishes our sonship with God the Father.

Often we find ourselves turning to that great field of music, the spiritual, for the gospel in homespun. Certainly there is one spiritual that needs to be sung in this day—it is "Everybody Talkin' 'Bout Heaven Ain't Goin' There." Not everyone becomes a son of God today. Just because we are members of the human family does not grant us the position whereby we can say, "Our Father." As the young couple had to turn away from the little lad at the orphanage, so God has to turn His back on a person who does not come the blood route—the way He has outlined. I know these are days of slipshod thinking, when sentiment passes current for the gospel, but God has fixed just one way!

We are living in a day of beauty-parlor religion. We settle for bubble-bath salvation instead of being plunged beneath the crimson flow that washes white as snow. We have mouthwash conversions instead of becoming new creations in Christ Jesus. We wear toothpaste smiles on our faces instead of the joy of the Lord in our hearts. We talk more about halo shampoo than about the fullness of the Holy Spirit. We give talcum-powder testimonies rather than those saturated with the fragrance of Christ. We live rosewater lives rather than lives manifesting the life of the Rose of Sharon. There is lipstick redemption instead of the precious blood of Christ. Synthetic jewelry is being worn instead of adorning the gospel of grace. And the glamour of Hollywood is being substituted for the glory of the holiness of God.

We must rise above the sham and come to an understanding of the fact that everyone is not a son of God. We can become His son in only one way. Think of it: even Nicodemus—a Pharisee with a God-given religion, a moral man, a man under Judaism who stood head and shoulders above everyone else—could not call God "Father." The Lord Jesus said to him, "Unless one is born again, he cannot see the kingdom of God" (John 3:3 NKJV). And in his Gospel, John said:

> **But as many as received Him, to them He gave the right** [or, even better, the *authority*, for that is the meaning of the word] **to become children of God, to those who believe in His name.** (John 1:12 NKJV)

My friend, is this first statement, "Our Father," your precious possession for use in prayer? Can you rightfully use it before the Throne? Is He your Father through faith in Jesus Christ?

. . . IN HEAVEN . . .

One of my many moments of being spiritually thrilled comes upon examining the second statement, "in heaven." But to be correctly translated it should read "in the heavens," for it is plural, not singular. While it was the custom in the New Testament to use the plural for the word *heaven*, it was not always the rule. When you drop down to Matthew 6:10 it reads, "Your kingdom come. Your will be done on earth as it is in heaven," and here it is in the singular and means the heaven of heavens, where God's throne is. But in the opening statement, the word is in the plural: "in the heavens." How wonderful that is!

And why is this so wonderful? There are three heavens mentioned in Scripture. The first was identified by the Lord Himself when He spoke of the birds of the heavens—the airspaces. These, then, are the first heaven. Then we read in Scripture of the stars of heaven—the stellar spaces that make up the second heaven. And finally, out in the vastness of His space somewhere is the throne of God—the third heaven. Paul spoke of being caught up into the third heaven. So, then, this prayer tells us that He is "our Father in the heavens"—the first heaven, the second heaven, and the very Throne of God itself. How that thrills us! It is the answer to man's wisdom today. I trust that some of the wonder and glory of this is beginning to break in upon your heart.

Greek philosophy projected several theories, one of which was atheism. This was based upon the premise that there is no God back of this universe. This prayer tells us that back of this universe there *is* a God and He is "our Father in the heavens." Back of creation there stands a personality—*God!*

Several years ago, an astronomer, speaking before an astronomers' association in London, called attention to a mass of new findings that revealed an ever-expanding universe. Then he commented, "In comparison to this universe—astronomically speaking—what is man?" A very scholarly, godly member of the body arose and said, "Sir, man is the astronomer." Man, living here on this earth, has looked out into space and, somehow, come to a workable understanding of it. But the great Architect and Creator, "our Father in the heavens," looks down upon man in his feeble attempt to understand the creation by some physical means.

Then there is the pernicious philosophy of pantheism abroad today. It goes by several names, but it is a philosophy holding that creation is the sum total of God—that there is no God other than the combined forces and laws manifested in the existing universe. Therefore, its followers worship the sea, the moon, the sun, and every other material thing in nature. To them, God is matter—the sum total of everything. But this prayer says, "Our Father in the heavens." He is not a prisoner in this universe. He is beyond and above it. He is in the airspaces, in the stellar spaces, but He is far removed from His universe today—He is more than creation! He is the One sitting upon the Throne of the universe, and He has it under His control!

And still another philosophy appears; it is known as deism. This system teaches that while God created this universe, He just wound it up as you do a clock and then went off and left it to take care of itself. Yes, it is true that He is beyond space upon the Throne of the universe. Proverbs says that God is far from the wicked, and David, being mindful of this, was continually in prayer: "O Lord, do not be far from me" (Psalm 35:22 NKJV).

But Scripture also tells us that He is a very present help in time of trouble. How glorious it is that this One, who is the Creator of the universe, came to this earth and in His redeeming work went to the cross, rose from the dead, and is today at God's right hand. But listen as He says, "Lo, I am with you always, even to the end of the age" (Matthew 28:20 NKJV), and "I will never leave you nor forsake you" (Hebrews 13:5 NKJV). For where two or three are gathered in His name, He is there (see Matthew 18:20). He is the omnipresent God, but at the same time He is ever present to help us as we face life with its problems and burdens.

. . . HALLOWED BE YOUR NAME

Now let us turn to the last great statement made in the introduction: "Hallowed be Your name." More correctly translated, it should read, "Let Your name be made holy." The name of God stands for all that God is. When the Lord was leading the children of Israel out of Egypt through the wilderness, He sent His angel and told them, "I want you to obey Moses; do what he tells you because My name is in him" (see Exodus 23:21). That means all that God is—all that God stands for—is in His name.

There is a very interesting verse in Leviticus: "And whoever blasphemes the name of the LORD shall surely be put to death" (24:16 NKJV). The name of God was so revered by the children of Israel that they did not even pronounce it. Consequently, no one knows today the pronunciation of that mystical tetragrammaton, YHWH. We have it translated "Jehovah"—some say it is "Yahweh"—who is right? No one knows! And why do we not know? Because the name of God was so holy, so sacred, and demanded such reverence that the children of Israel dared not even speak it.

In conservative circles today there is a familiarity with the name of God that ought not to be. You and I become too familiar with things that are sacred and holy, and we need to be very careful in this. It is tragic when a man or woman out on the street takes God's name in vain—but the thing that is more tragic is the blasphemy of the sanctuary. And do you know what that is? It is the thing of which I am continually reminding myself. We who walk into the pulpit do so with such frequency that we become familiar with it. We can brush against holy and sacred things so constantly that they can become commonplace. When a guest speaker comes to our pulpit, I always observe his manner as he approaches the sacred desk. And you who come to the pew—you do well to be reverent in His presence in the house that has been dedicated to Him. God, deliver us from treating as commonplace the things that are sacred before You!

But let us think upon the way in which you and I can make God's name holy. Can we add to that which is already infinitely holy? Certainly not. Then what did our Lord mean by the statement, "Hallowed be Your name"? We are sure that He meant more than that we should arise in some Sunday morning service and repeat with the others, "Hallowed be Your name." He meant that by our lives we are to make God's name holy.

There are two men whose names are mentioned in Genesis: one commended the name of God, and the other was a disgrace to the name of God. These two men had one characteristic in common—they always built an altar where they chose to dwell. When Abraham went into Canaan, a Canaanite passing by observed that he had a new neighbor for he had seen his altar. Everywhere Abraham went, he built an altar to God. And Abraham began to do business with the Canaanites, who found him to be honest. They found that everything Abraham said invited their confidence. Finally they reached the conclusion that the God whom Abraham worshiped was a holy God, and surely the name of God was made holy in Canaan because of the life of Abraham.

But when Jacob started out, he could not be trusted. Do not attempt to explain away the first part of his life, for it held only dishonor. Two things always marked the path over which he had gone: he had built an altar and he had defrauded someone. One day God met him as he was en route—he was alone and God led him down by the brook Jabbok. And God made it clear to Jacob that he could not continue conducting himself in that manner, for God's name must be made holy. And God caused the socket of Jacob's leg to be dislocated. I believe that God will do that today for any one of His children who is bringing dishonor to His name.

Paul said to his people in that day, "The name of God is blasphemed among the Gentiles because of you" (Romans 2:24 NKJV). My fundamental friend, my premillennial brother, let us go to the top of yonder mountain where He gave the Sermon on the Mount—we need to go there. We must have men and women who name the name of God and whose lives correspond to it!

I commented to a friend of mine, "If I ever leave the ministry—and there are times when I am tempted to do it—it will not be due to a loss of faith in the Book." There was a time when I had doubts about the Bible, but today I do not have a single doubt; I am willing to stake the eternal destiny of my soul upon the accuracy of the Bible. I believe it with all my heart. If I ever leave the ministry, it will be because of leaders who profess to know the name of God but blaspheme that name in their living.

Go to the top of the mountain and listen as He reveals His will. I know we are not saved by the Sermon on the Mount, but you and I can make His name holy by reading it and abiding therein. I know it is a ministry of condemnation, but it will cause us to flee to Jesus for refuge, for salvation, deliverance, and power; and we will become God's child by faith in Jesus Christ that we might be enabled to make His name holy in our living. Are you hallowing God's name in your daily life?

GOD'S COMING
KINGDOM ON THE EARTH

IN THUMBING THROUGH HISTORY'S PAGES, ONE must remain at length in the reading of the fabulous nineteenth century—better known as the Victorian Era—for it was in this period, under the reign of Queen Victoria, that the British Empire came to its great expansion through colonization. This was, in truth, the Golden Age. Scientific accomplishments gave impetus to the times, and science began to prophesy that it would bring in a new world order, a new age.

Out of so promising a background, the twentieth century was born in high hopes and aspirations. Perhaps there was never a more propitious time for high ideals and dreams than the opening of the twentieth century. With a fanfare of trumpets, it moved upon the scene. Optimism was the dominant note of the hour. Man was going forth in that day as a knight clad in shining armor. "Onward and upward forever" was the catchphrase of the new day. Just around the corner was the millennial kingdom—coming to pass *ipso facto*—for man had willed it and had made the world a glorious place!

Now the church, quick to catch the spirit of the age and permeated with this leaven of false hope, spoke bravely of converting the world. In the writings of the year 1901 lie an interesting bit of reading on the Lord's Prayer. Listen to this kind of daydreaming:

> The Prayer, thus taught us, gives faith and hope that His kingdom is coming. The sun's dawning rays on the mountain tops are the assurance that the perfect day will come. The best things in individuals and in nations, increasing each decade, are proof of their final prevalence![1]

Further, we note that the Student Volunteer Movement of 1912 had as its motto: "The World for Christ in this Generation." In later years, a minister identified with this movement told me, "It is hard for me today to realize that at that time we actually believed that the world would be won for Christ within the next few years."

There was a great missionary emphasis in the early part of the twentieth century. Africa, China, and Japan were open fully to the gospel, and inroads were made for the cause of Christ everywhere throughout the world. About that same time, a Peace Conference was held at the Hague in Holland. At this conference men wore little plowshares made out of swords upon the lapels of their coats. "There will never be another war," they said. "There will be a war-less world—we are coming into a new day."

It is difficult for us today to relate to the thinking of men in that day. Postmillennialism was in the saddle, and riding mankind was a push toward "building the kingdom." In fact, the church was made synonymous with the kingdom in that day. But frankly, any suggestion of the coming of Jesus Christ would have been a source of great embarrassment, as His coming would only have interfered with the accomplishments of men, holding up the glorious program they had for self-improvement of the race. Men who were premillennial and did speak of the coming of Christ were looked down upon—they were considered strange individuals. And strange seemed the messages of such men as Dr. Brooks, Dr. Wilbur Chapman, Dr. Morehouse, and Dr. Torrey. In his introduction to Dr. W. E. Blackstone's little book, *Jesus Is Coming,* Dr. Torrey stated how difficult it was to preach the precious hope in days when popular opinion would have agreed that the sweeping successes of man would surely bring in the kingdom.

But there has come a great change! In the race today, all the way from statesman down to the humblest ranks, people are disappointed, discouraged, distraught, and disillusioned. What has happened since the dawn of the twentieth century? An inventory includes wars the likes of which the world had never seen. A worldwide depression swept over us, and today a godless ideology threatens Christianity. Science is no longer the savior of the race but the destroyer.

In the world of the spiritual, postmillennialism is as dead as a dodo bird. You will not find on the topside of the earth today a reputable theologian who is postmillennial. Now that does not mean that they have become premillennial—they have not. They have become amillennial. They have given up the idea of the Millennium altogether because they have come to the conclusion that they are not getting the contract from God to build the kingdom of heaven here upon this earth.

YOUR KINGDOM COME . . .

An idealistic character in Robert Browning's poem, "Pippa Passes," sings forth the spirit of the nineteenth century:

> The year's at the spring
> And day's at the morn;
> Morning's at seven;
> The hillside's dew-pearled,
> The lark's on the wing;
> The snail's on the thorn:
> God's in his heaven
> All's right with the world![2]

But in our present day I fear we shall have to turn to Shakespeare's *Hamlet* for a summary of our age of confusion. It is there that we find the line, "Something is rotten in the state of Denmark."[3]

There is something definitely wrong in this world in which we live. In spite of that, however, men are still talking bravely about building the kingdom. But, my friend, they are conducting a bankruptcy sale on a new world order and a fire sale on a new social order. I am of the same opinion as Dr. George Guille, who said that it seems as if the church is in the business of making the world a better place for men to go to hell in. Yes, the church was engaged, and feverishly so, in its program for making the world religious when it suddenly became infatuated with an idea that greatly expanded its program—namely, that the church could and would bring the kingdom of God here on this earth.

Now this term *kingdom* causes, I suppose, more confusion than any other term in Scripture. What meaning is wrapped up in that word? I do not want to appear too dogmatic where good men differ, but there are certain basic principles that we can state. And I would like the liberty of making this personal observation. For years I thought that the Old Testament and the Epistles were difficult since they contained doctrine. But I thought the Gospels were simple and, in a measure, quite easy to comprehend. May I say to you that I have arrived at the conclusion that the Old Testament and the Epistles are simple, while the most difficult portion of the Word of God is the Gospels. It is in the Gospels that we find the theme song, "The Kingdom."

Now if I can make clear to you something of what this kingdom means, it will help you, I believe, more than any other one thing to get a correct perspective of the Word of God and of life. Basically, mention of the kingdom lies in the Old Testament. When John the Baptist appeared with the Lord Jesus Christ, they began with the message: "Repent, for the kingdom of heaven is at hand." Now, neither the Lord Jesus nor John explained it; neither shed any light upon it in the sense of attempting to define it. This argues that the people to whom they were speaking understood what they meant. It is that kingdom that, at first, had been vouchsafed to David, of which God said to him, "I'll bring One to sit on your throne, I'll bring the Messiah, and He will reign in righteousness and justice and peace on this earth" (see 2 Samuel 7:12–17).

The prophets took up this song and sang it in the dark hours of the night. A day was coming when Jerusalem would become the very center of this earth—the Capital City, if you please. It was the bright ray of hope in the darkest hour of these people. They sang that the entire earth would be ruled over by this One who was to come. Even nature would be affected. The desert would blossom as the rose. The sun, moon, and stars would be affected. Just as the events that took place in Bethlehem made it outshine all the other thousands of cities of Judah, so is this little planet of ours made the jewel of the great universe of God—for here is where the glory of God was to break!

May I say that this kingdom is a progressive and growing thing. Isaiah said:

Of the increase of His government and peace there will be no end, upon the throne of David and over His king-

dom, to order it and establish it with judgment and jus-tice from that time forward, even forever. The zeal of the LORD of hosts will perform this. (Isaiah 9:7 NKJV)

My own point of view—and like many McGee theories, it may not be too good—is that this kingdom will increase and grow throughout eternity. That is going to be one of the glories of it. There will be nothing static or sterile about this kingdom at all; it will be characterized by constant growth! And I think it is defined in our petition, "Your kingdom come."

YOUR WILL BE DONE ON EARTH AS IT IS IN HEAVEN

"Your will be done on earth as it is in heaven." What did the Lord Jesus mean as He gave this petition? Is it that the will of God, which is all-prevailing in heaven, shall ultimately prevail here upon this earth? Yes, His glory will shine forth on this earth! It is God's intention that His will shall some-day prevail here where rebellion has broken out and man lives in sin and unbelief. May I give you just one verse out of many found in the Old Testament:

And in the days of these kings the God of heaven will set up a kingdom which shall never be destroyed; and the kingdom shall not be left to other people; it shall break in pieces and consume all these kingdoms, and it shall stand forever. (Daniel 2:44 NKJV)

That is the kingdom toward which God is moving.

While this kingdom is not altogether spiritual, it has a spiritual aspect. Some will say, "Yes, but you know the Bible says that the kingdom of God is not meat or drink but righteousness, peace, and joy in the Holy Spirit." Let me illustrate my point: the Preamble to the Constitution of these United States says that we are given freedom for the pursuit of happiness. It does not guarantee happiness, but it guarantees the right to pursue it in liberty. Now happiness, while an abstract term, is spiritual and is to be sought by us while we are in a physical world of mountains, rivers, seacoasts, deserts, plains, and valleys. With this in mind, let us go back to the thought of the kingdom.

> *For the kingdom of God is not eating and drinking, but righteousness and peace and joy in the Holy Spirit.*
> (Romans 14:17 NKJV)

That righteousness is to cover the earth as the waters cover the sea, and it is a peace that *only* He, who is the Prince of Peace, can bring to this earth!

This brings us to the all-important question: is the church part of this kingdom? The Lord Jesus said, "My kingdom is not of this world" (John 18:36 NKJV). Someone will reply, "Now you see, it does not pertain to down here." Yes, but He said the same thing concerning believers—that they are *in* this world but not *of* it. His kingdom is to be in this world, but it is not to be established by the world's methods.

It is not moved forward by the politics of this world. His kingdom will contain no Republican or Democratic platform. It will be established and maintained on a different basis from that of our world.

Again we ask the question: is the church part of this kingdom? Some of my good brethren say that the answer is no. So I want to be very careful at this point. When you say that the church is not the kingdom, I think you are accurate; but when you say that the church is not *part* of the kingdom, then I think you are wrong. May I illustrate: California is part of the United States, but California is not the United States. Nor is the church the kingdom; it is merely *part* of the kingdom. And how does she become a part of the kingdom? Well, she will be the bride of the King of that kingdom.

Therefore, let us consider again the laws under which the bride must live in that new kingdom. They are to be found in the Sermon on the Mount. The church—the bride to be—is now under grace, living under new principles by the Holy Spirit. But that does not mean that she can flout the Sermon on the Mount and despise it. Come, my fundamental friend, my premillennial brother, and let us, as members of that church, go once again up to the top of that mountain where He gave the sermon. Let us look into His face. We need to, you know. This is His law. I know that we are not under law, but—at the same time—we do not despise law. He values honor and integrity. Faithfulness and righteousness are things that He counts as valuable. And, my friend, purity still counts in the high court of heaven. How we have dipped our colors and come to the place in fundamental circles where we close our eyes to these things that we need to recognize.

But the kingdom that is mentioned in Scripture—the one that we pray about—is coming in glory. It is that glorious kingdom that shall be established someday on this earth—His millennial kingdom. The kingdom in creation, the whole creation, is groaning and travailing, waiting for the day; even we, ourselves, are awaiting that day, for "it has not yet been revealed what we shall be, but we know that when He is revealed, we shall be like Him" (1 John 3:2 NKJV). The King will be revealed, His glory will be extended on this earth, and righteousness and peace will cover this earth as the waters cover the sea.

Our prayer looks even beyond the millennial kingdom. "Your kingdom come." Whose kingdom? "Our Father in heaven, *Your* kingdom come"—that eternal kingdom that is mentioned in 1 Corinthians 15 where we are given an order and a development of the kingdom. Let us notice it briefly:

> **But now Christ is risen from the dead, and has become the firstfruits of those who have fallen asleep.** (1 Corinthians 15:20 NKJV)

He is back from the dead, and after Him those that are His are going to arise. He is merely the firstfruits. And then we read:

> **Then comes the end, when He delivers the kingdom to God the Father, when He puts an end to all rule and all authority and power.** (1 Corinthians 15:24 NKJV)

Does that mean that the millennial kingdom is coming to an end? Oh, no, it is an everlasting kingdom. What shall be happening is revealed in the following:

> **Now when all things are made subject to Him, then the Son Himself will also be subject to Him who put all things under Him, that God may be all in all.** (1 Corinthians 15:28 NKJV)

After the Lord Jesus reigns on this earth for one thousand years, after Satan is put down eternally, after the lost have been judged—He returns to His place in the Godhead that God may be all in all. But He will continue to reign and this earth will continue to be the kingdom and the place of blessing. This is the day of His rejection; this is the day when men turn their backs upon Him. His glory is not manifested today, but it is a time when you and I can bow to His scepter. Everything is sweeping toward that kingdom.

Do you have a passion for His kingdom? Are you looking forward to His coming in glory? It is that kingdom spoken of in Revelation 21 and 22—a kingdom in which there will be no tears, no death, no sorrow, no pain, and no fear. I ask you, are you looking forward to it? Today you and I can say, "Your will be done on earth," if our hopes and longings are bound up in this blessed thought.

Now the church is in the very heart of His program as He is sweeping events toward that glorious kingdom. Are you moving forward with Him? I think God's great men of the past moved with Him. When John Knox said, "Give me Scotland or I die," he was praying, I think, "Your kingdom come. Your will be done on earth as it is in heaven." When the Puritans came to this country and established a place where they could worship God and propagate the gospel of Christ, they were saying, in fact, if not in word, "Your kingdom come. Your will be done on earth as it is in heaven." And there are times when you and I arise to that high level and say from our hearts, when a passion is there, that His will might prevail here on this earth.

This part of the Lord's Prayer—"Your kingdom come"— is corporate, I believe. It speaks of the global purpose of God in this world. "Your will be done on earth as it is in heaven" has, I think, a personal angle. When we say it, we are pledging allegiance to Him. This makes it difficult for a sleek, sophisticated congregation to repeat it in a very glib way on Sunday morning.

Paul was a son of God, and he exalted that truth. He gloried in the fact that by regeneration he had come into the place of sonship. "Paul, a bondservant of Jesus Christ . . ." (Romans 1:1 NKJV), he wrote of himself. Paul, a prisoner of Jesus Christ! Yes, I also am a son of God; but I must bow to His scepter if I want His will done in my life. I am His prisoner. Christ is King, and He wears the crown and holds the scepter. He is the greatest of dictators. He wants your body, your heart, your mind, your soul—He wants *you*. In these days of His rejection, have you bowed to Him? If not, do not dare say, "Your kingdom come. Your will be done on earth as it is in heaven."

God's Word yields a beautiful incident, the knowledge of which brings a demand for decision on our part. The story lies in the days of David's rejection. David was God's anointed king, but Saul was pressing him hard so that he had to leave the throne, Jerusalem, and even his kingdom. He went across the Jordan River and camped there. David had on guard one of his own men to watch at the banks of the Jordan, though the river was at flood stage. Suddenly the guard ran to David with the message, "There are men swimming the Jordan over toward us." David went down to the water's edge and said to the strangers, "If you come peaceably, your heart will be knit to me. But if you come to do me harm, I will do you harm." And these men lifted their voices as best they could while swimming against the current and said, "Oh, David, we want to join you." When they got to the other side, exhausted from swimming against the current, they fell down before David. And Amasai said, "We are yours, O David; we are on your side, O son of Jesse!" (See 1 Chronicles 12:15–18.)

This is the day of Christ's rejection. If you want to bow to Him, you must swim against the currents of this world. If you are going to yield to Him today, you will go contrary to

GIVE US THIS DAY
OUR DAILY BREAD

THE AVERAGE WELL-GROOMED, WELL-FED Christian congregation of the day will find it very difficult to repeat seriously the petition, "Give us this day our daily bread." Someone has defined the average church service in America today as a service in which a mild-mannered man gets up before a group of mild-mannered people and urges them to be more mild-mannered. What a sad commentary that is upon the church, if that be true!

But it is very difficult for Americans, who go out to great supermarkets and push baskets through a maze of shelves groaning with all kinds of foodstuffs, to ask God for bread. God just does not seem to be in the colossal business of mass merchandising today. Why make fervent prayer to God for bread in this day of the welfare state, when we are looking to government instead of looking to God? This is a time when we are trying to detour around God in order to get our bread. We have come to a time when statism is a menace. Rome, with her excesses and welfare program, should be a danger signal before us in our day. What can follow in the wake of such a program but immorality and decay?

In America at this hour, there is plenty; but this is the only nation where there is plenty, yes, even a surplus today. Famine stalks this world today in many parts—the third horseman of the Apocalypse is riding, even now, across the land. We are living on an earth that has the curse of sin upon it. From the day that Adam sinned, God said to him:

> *In the sweat of your face you shall eat bread.* (Genesis 3:19 NKJV)

And from that day until the present hour, men have found no magic process of producing bread other than by hard work.

We may have it easy now, but may I say that there is a day coming when men in this country will be able to pray this prayer with a great deal of anxiety, of seeking, asking, and knocking—"Give us this day our daily bread."

Now, I want you to notice this petition for a moment. It is so simple, and yet it should come from our hearts with great enthusiasm. It speaks of our utter dependence upon God. Our bodily wants, our physical necessities, all come from Him, and He supplies them day by day. Israel gathered manna for the day; they gathered nothing for the morrow. They were not permitted to keep manna for the next week. This prayer, "Give us this day our daily bread," shows man that he lives from hand to mouth and that even his bodily necessities, his basic needs, come from God.

When we pray, "Give us this day our daily bread," we are asking God for those basic needs of our physical bodies, and it should teach us to depend upon God and rest upon Him. May I say that I do not think a Christian should be alarmed today because of what the economist is saying about diminishing resources. We are not looking to man to supply our needs; we are looking to God. We must learn to acknowledge God in all the affairs of our lives. A little poem that we teach our children expresses this well:

> Said the robin to the sparrow,
> "I should really like to know
> Why these anxious human beings
> Rush about and worry so!"
> Said the sparrow to the robin,
> "Friend, I think that it must be
> That they have no Heavenly Father
> Such as cares for you and me!"[1]

You and I need to remember what He has told us in His Word: when we put Him first, all these other things—these necessities—will be added unto us (see Matthew 6:33).

There is another thing in this simple petition, "Give us this day our daily bread." God is the giver of everything. You will not find His price on the loaf of bread that you buy—He is on the giving side. As you look at the loaf of bread on your table, let the thought be thankfully with you that the bread has come ultimately from the hand of God.

Back of the loaf is the snowy flour; and back of the flour,
the mill; and back of the mill is the wheat and the shower,
the sun, and the Father's will.[2]

Back of that loaf of bread is our generous Father, and we can
say to Him, "Give us this day our daily bread."

Now, I believe that the Lord's Prayer will not reach its
full fruition until the Millennium comes. But someone will
ask the question, "How can they pray this petition during
the Millennium with the curse removed from the earth and
an abundance here?" I'll tell you how they can pray it, because in that day the One who fed the multitudes with the
loaves and fishes will feed His own. The prophet Isaiah said
that in that day, "He will feed His flock like a shepherd"
(Isaiah 40:11 NKJV), and in that day men will pray, "Give us
this day our daily bread."

But this prayer has for you and me a higher meaning than
that which is physical. For the Christian it has a spiritual as
well as a physical meaning. It is more than food, for "man
shall not live by bread alone" (Deuteronomy 8:3 NKJV). Man
has been created for something greater than that, though this
little poem does portray some folk in this world:

> Into this world to eat and sleep
> And know no reason why he was born
> Save only to consume the corn,
> Devour the cattle, flock and fish,
> And leave behind an empty dish.[3]

That is about all some folk do, just satisfy their physical needs and live like animals. But no child of God is here to live in that fashion. We are called to something higher than that, and the food that is spoken of here is spiritual food. This has a spiritual meaning for Christians, for they have not been promised physical blessings alone. Physical blessings are secondary to the Christian today. But if you have them, then thank God, remembering that they are extras. David said:

> *I have been young, and now am old; yet I have not seen the righteous forsaken, nor his descendants begging bread.* (Psalm 37:25 NKJV)

But I guarantee you, there are believers today "begging bread." Beloved, may I say to you, God has not promised us physical blessings. He has promised us *spiritual* blessings. Material blessings were promised and given to the nation Israel, but spiritual blessings have been promised to the church. If you want another distinction between Israel in the Old Testament and the church in the New Testament, then remember: physical blessings in the Old Testament; spiritual blessings in the New Testament.

When Paul the apostle was converted, he was not given a book recommending all of the choice places in which to eat in the Roman Empire. When Paul listed the things that he suffered, he said, "We both hunger and thirst" (1 Corinthians 4:11 NKJV). He knew what it was to hunger. And God's children down through the ages have known what it is to actually go without food. They have known hunger for physical food. The full story has never been told of the thousands who starved to death in Europe during World War II—many of them Christians. There were endless numbers of Christian families in which the father and mother bowed their heads in the mornings and would say, "Give us this day our daily bread," and then they would see their little ones waste away. Finally death would come to the children, and the parents would look at this petition and wonder what was its meaning.

My friend, as a Christian, you must explain to people what this petition means. To tell them that it means physical bread would be all wrong. God did not say that we would not suffer in this age, but He did say that He would provide spiritual bread today for those who want it and who know their need of it. The psalmist told us that when Israel complained to God and wanted meat to eat, God gave them quails. And the psalmist said, "And He gave them their request, but sent leanness into their soul" (Psalm 106:15 NKJV). And today God does not always grant our requests, because He does not want our souls to be lean. God is providing us a spiritual bread, for He said,

Blessed are those who hunger and thirst for righteousness, for they shall be filled. (Matthew 5:6 NKJV)

Do you have a hunger and thirst that the world cannot satisfy? Do you thirst after righteousness? I point you to the One who said:

I am the bread of life. He who comes to Me shall never hunger, and he who believes in Me shall never thirst. (John 6:35 NKJV)

Do you know what it is to have your spiritual thirst slaked? Do you know what it is to have that deep-down hunger in your heart satisfied by coming to the One who is the Bread of Life? Oh, today, may our prayer be: "Give us this day our daily bread." May our hearts go out to Him, for He said:

If anyone thirsts, let him come to Me and drink. (John 7:37 NKJV)

There is a verse in the Psalms that has meant a great deal to me, and I want to pass it on to you. It is in Psalm 104, which opens with "Bless the LORD, O my soul!" And verse 15 (NKJV) reads as follows:

. . . And wine that makes glad the heart of man, oil to make his face shine, and bread which strengthens man's heart.

This is not bread for the stomach, oil just for the physical face, and wine of the world. Rather, it is the joy of the Lord, the fullness of the Spirit, and the Bread—the Lord Jesus—that satisfy the heart of man.

Is He all of this today in your heart and life?

FORGIVENESS, TEMPTATION, AND DELIVERANCE

IN AN EARLIER CHAPTER I STATED THAT THE Lord's Prayer falls into seven petitions: three pertaining to God, or those known as "the theocentric petitions," and four that are manward and are known as "the anthropocentric petitions." It is the latter group—those having to do with the foundational and fundamental things in our lives—that we wish to focus on at this time. They deal with that ugly thing called *sin*. It was Charles Spurgeon who said that no prayer of mortal man could be complete without a confession of sin, and this part of the Lord's Prayer faces up to this business of sin, the reality of it, and how to handle it. One of the things that marks us today is that we will not face up to reality. Not only is it true of the isms, but it is true of many individually. We want to deal with things that are theoretical—not with things that are actual. But this prayer is real and actual.

AND FORGIVE US OUR DEBTS, AS WE FORGIVE OUR DEBTORS

I want you to note these three wordings: "And forgive us our debts, as we forgive our debtors," is Matthew's account of it. If you turn to Luke 11:4 (NKJV) you will find that it is: "And forgive us our sins, for we also forgive everyone who is indebted to us." It was Tyndale in his translation who brought forth the word *trespass,* and you will find in some churches today where there is formal religion, liturgy, and ritual, the use of "forgive us our debts," while others will use "forgive us our trespasses." Two little girls were talking about the Lord's Prayer as repeated in their churches. One said, "We have trespasses in our church," and the other said, "Well, in our church we have debts," and they were both probably right as far as the churches of our day are concerned—they have both debts and trespasses!

Which one is accurate? There is no difficulty here at all since all of these words refer to the same thing, and that thing is sin. In Scripture there are many words for sin. Sin is a complicated and mysterious thing. Goodness and virtue are simple. One of the things that is attractive about sin is that it is like a maze or a puzzle; it is something that you do not know too much about. Let us turn to an illustration for this thought. If I were to hold a straight stick behind my back and ask ten people to draw a picture of it, I have a notion that they all would draw just about the same kind of picture—it would be straight. Now that represents goodness—it is always just one way, and it cannot be two ways. But if I held a crooked stick behind me and asked ten more people to draw a picture of it, I have a notion that there would be as many different pictures of that crooked stick as persons drawing it. That represents sin. Sin can be crooked in a million different ways; Scripture, therefore, uses many different words for it.

It would be of interest to look at some of those words. It is called "debt" because it is a debt to God. It is called "missing the mark" because we fall short of the glory of God. It is called "lawlessness," "disobedience," "trespass," "crossing the boundary," or "a moral aberration." Then there are such terms as "impiety," "blasphemy," and "disharmony," meaning that which is out of harmony with God. These are some of the words that are used to set forth sin in all of its complexity today. There are sins of omission as well as sins of commission. We say we have done what we should not have done, but we have left undone those things that we should have done. But they all may be crystallized into one meaning in the use of the word *debt*—something that we owe. Today you and I are in debt to God. We owe Him something, and we have not paid that obligation; we have not discharged our responsibility.

"And forgive us our debts [our sins], as we forgive our debtors [those who are indebted to us]." This is on a legalistic basis and, frankly, I am rather afraid to pray the prayer just like that. It was a Puritan theologian who made the statement that to pray the prayer with an unforgiving spirit means in actuality to say, "God, do not forgive me because I do not forgive those who are around me." How many people there are today of whom that would be true! They have an unforgiving spirit, and yet they have the audacity to say to God, "Forgive me as I forgive those round about me."

If God forgave us as we forgive those round about us, I fear that few of us would ever be forgiven. For in the heart of man there is an unforgiving spirit. David committed a grave sin, and God said to him, "You are to be punished, David. But I will let you choose your punishment. Would you prefer to fall into the hands of God or into the hands of your enemy?" It did not take David long to arrive at a conclusion in that matter, for he cried out to God, "Oh, let me fall into the hands of God, for He is merciful, and let me not fall into the hands of man." (See 2 Samuel 24:10–14.)

I am grateful that I do not have to stand before my enemies in judgment. I often receive many kind letters in response to my ministry, but every now and then I receive a harsh and critical letter—and how distressing it is. It is difficult to see how it could have come from the heart of a Christian. And when I read a letter like that, I am glad that I do not have to stand before that person in judgment, for I would not stand a chance. Perhaps he ought to be thankful that he will not have to stand before me, because he might not get off so easy either. You see, we would not be very gracious to each other. We are not even gracious to ourselves. We sometimes hear the expression, "I wanted to kick myself." God has no such attitude toward you. David said,

"Let me fall into the hands of God—He is merciful—and let me not fall into the hands of my enemies." That is grace. "And forgive us our debts, as we forgive our debtors" is not grace—it is legalistic.

I thank God for another verse of Scripture:

> *And be kind to one another, tenderhearted, forgiving one another, even as God in Christ forgave you.* (Ephesians 4:32 NKJV)

Today God is forgiving us on the basis of what Christ has done for us, not on the basis by which we forgive. The redemption of God is in full view when God forgives us. It does not refer to our salvation when we read, "And forgive us our debts, as we forgive our debtors." He is speaking there to those who are already saved and have the nature of God. He does not wait for you to forgive before He forgives. That is not His method of settling the sin question. He gave His Son to die, and it is on that basis that God forgives and saves.

Do you know that it is more difficult for God to forgive sin than it is for you or me to forgive infringements? I can make this clear with a homely illustration. If you should step on my shoe and spoil my shine and then say to me, "I am sorry, will you forgive me?" I would say, "Sure. I was going to have another shine anyhow. Forget it." But it is a vastly different matter when we watch a judge who is trying a criminal. He should not let that criminal go free just because he expresses sorrow for his act. The judge is in the position of being a ruler and is obligated to uphold the law. So it would be more difficult for the judge to forgive than for me to forgive you for having spoiled my shine as you stepped on my shoe.

Let us follow this thought a little further. God is the moral ruler of this universe in which you and I live, and when He forgives He cannot do it by just letting down the bars and taking us into the back door of heaven. But to return to our illustration: suppose that a criminal was condemned to death, and we decided to call upon the governor of the state to forestall any efforts to delay the carrying out of the sentence. If this criminal met us at the door of the governor's mansion, we would be startled and naturally ask him: "What in the world are you doing here?" Should he reply, "Haven't you heard? The governor has pardoned me and brought me as a guest to his home!" then we would know that some conniving had taken place somewhere. If God would forgive you in like manner, then He would be compromising with sin and would be admitting criminals into heaven. God cannot do that. Do not think that God forgives on some little sentimental basis, that somehow He shuts His eyes to the sin question. The teaching that God forgives sin without doing anything about it is liberalism at its very core. Yes, God forgives sin, but He has to do something about it.

Again let us return to our illustration. Suppose, if upon meeting this criminal at the governor's door, he should say to you, "Haven't you heard? The governor's son has paid the penalty for my sin, and the governor is going to adopt me as his son—he is going to give me the rights of citizenship, is going to take this fallen nature out of me and make me a law-abiding citizen." Would you approve that? Well, that is exactly what God has done about the sin question. God forgives only on one basis: His Son came into this world, went to the cross, and paid the full penalty for your sin and my sin. Today we have forgiveness with Him because He paid the debt and set us free. In the death of Christ upon the cross our sins have been removed "as far as the east is from the west" (Psalm 103:12 NKJV)—He has put them where He remembers them no more.

There is a mercy seat today for the sinner. We recall the poor tax collector who stood afar off, beat upon his chest, and said, "God, be merciful to me a sinner!" (Luke 18:13 NKJV). What he actually said was, "Lord, be mercy-seated to me." The mercy seat in the temple of God was beyond the tax collector, and he was denied access to it. As far as he was concerned, there was no forgiveness for him at all. Therefore, he cried out to God in desperation. Today, there is a mercy seat for everyone—it is the blood of Christ. That is made the throne of judgment, the throne of grace, and we can come before Him boldly and find help.

This petition of the Lord's Prayer is for those who have been born again and have the nature of God. It is for their lives and service, and so it is very pertinent and practical. Along the shoreline of Christian work there is wreck after wreck of those who were one time in Christian service and are out today for one reason: they have an unforgiving spirit. Will you listen to the thing that John said in his first Epistle:

> *He who says he is in the light, and hates his brother, is in darkness until now. He who loves his brother abides in the light, and there is no cause for stumbling in him. But he who hates his brother is in darkness and walks in darkness, and does not know where he is going, because the darkness has blinded his eyes. I write to you, little children, because your sins are forgiven you for His name's sake.* (1 John 2:9–12 NKJV)

Remember this one thing: God has forgiven us through the blood of His Son. But on the basis of our forgiveness of one another are our service and walk conditioned. It is on that basis that we worship God. The Lord Jesus said that if you go to the altar and remember that your brother has anything against you, do not even go on with your worship, as important as that is, but leave it and go and be reconciled to your brother (see Matthew 5:23–24). That is of paramount importance. And how many times our Lord repeated this! Over in the Epistle to the Colossians Paul said it in just a little different way:

> *Therefore, as the elect of God, holy and beloved, put on tender mercies, kindness, humility, meekness, longsuffering; bearing with one another, and forgiving one another, if anyone has a complaint against another; even as*

Christ forgave you, so you also must do. (Colossians 3:12–13 NKJV)

Many people who claim to be fundamental in their faith are nursing little grudges; they are holding a hatred in their heart against a brother and having an unforgiving spirit. You know, Paul and Barnabas disagreed. Barnabas, the "Son of Encouragement" (Acts 4:36 NKJV), was not much encouragement to Paul when they disagreed over John Mark and were separated. But Paul was wrong about John Mark, and at the end of his ministry he recognized that. Paul said, "Get Mark and bring him with you, for he is useful to me for ministry" (2 Timothy 4:11 NKJV). What a wonderful spirit this man Paul had!

I have in my possession a very personal letter to Dr. R. A. Torrey written by Dr. Frank DeWitt Talmadge. This letter comes out of a day when men were giants on this earth. I came into possession of this letter while a pastor in Pasadena, California, at a church that had the desk and filing cabinet of Dr. Torrey. One day when I reached into his filing cabinet, which was filled with envelopes, I found that one envelope contained a letter dated January 2, 1900. It is from this that I give the following excerpt: "Dear Dr. Torrey: Today I'm standing under the shadow of two griefs. First, that of Mr. Moody's death; secondly, the fear that I may have done you a very great injustice." At this point he outlined what it was and then concluded—"If there is any way that I can rectify the wrong, I'll gladly do so." Then he told how he was willing to do it, and it was a way very humbling to him. Then he closed with this: "May the sweet spirit of Him who is gone make me more and more preach the Gospel of love. Yours, with sorrow, Frank DeWitt Talmadge." These men were giants, and they were big because they knew how to forgive. It is something all of us need today.

"And forgive us our debts, as we forgive our debtors." Do we forgive that He might harness us for service—that He might bless us richly? Great men, such as Paul, have a forgiving spirit. Those men, when wrong, acknowledge when they are wrong. One listens almost in vain today to hear some minister or Christian worker acknowledge that he is wrong. We are living in a day when no one is wrong and no one apologizes. How the church needs men and women who will humble themselves and ask forgiveness when they have wounded a brother!

AND DO NOT LEAD US INTO TEMPTATION . . .

Now let us look at the next petition: "And do not lead us into temptation." This word *lead* gives us the wrong impression, because James said God does not tempt any man (see James 1:13). A better translation here would be, "Do not leave us in temptation." It does not mean to keep us out of it, but when we are in it, not to leave us there.

In a church in the South some years ago, the preacher

called on the membership to stand and give a favorite verse. One deacon got up and said his favorite verse in the Scripture was "It came to pass." Everyone looked puzzled. Finally the preacher said, "Now look here, brother, what do you mean?" He answered, "I'll tell you. When I get into trouble, or I get into temptation, I always turn to that verse in the Bible where it says, 'It came to pass' and I say, 'Hallelujah! It came to pass—it didn't come to stay—and God will deliver me out of it.'"

My friend, that may be misusing Scripture, but I want to say that he was absolutely accurate. That is exactly what the Scripture says: "The Lord knows how to deliver the godly out of temptations" (2 Peter 2:9 NKJV). And again:

> *No temptation has overtaken you except such as is common to man; but God is faithful, who will not allow you to be tempted beyond what you are able, but with the temptation will also make the way of escape, that you may be able to bear it.* (1 Corinthians 10:13 NKJV)

If you have ever noticed a freight train as it was passing, you saw that each boxcar has on it "Net Weight." That means that each boxcar has a certain capacity, and they never let it get overloaded. Now God knows what your capacity is—He knows how much weight you can carry—and He will not let you be tempted above what you are able to handle.

. . . But Deliver Us from the Evil One

Finally: "But deliver us from the evil one." Satan is an awful reality. The world laughed at Martin Luther, who threw an inkwell at him. But recently we have had a turn in events. I suppose that one of the greatest brains of the world was C. S. Lewis, and in his book, *The Screwtape Letters,* he took apart the liberal who denies the reality of Satan. Any man who stands for God knows that Satan is real. As we work in any sort of Christian service, we become conscious of the presence of God and also dreadfully conscious of the presence of Satan. But we have this petition: "But deliver us from the evil one."

The reason most of us fall today is because we are in the wrong place. We are like the little boy sitting in the pantry and looking at the cookie jar. His mother called out, "Willie, where are you?" He said, "I'm in the pantry." Then she asked, "What are you doing in there?" He replied, "I'm fighting temptation." That is the distance most people choose in fighting temptation today! If a fast train passes through a station, those who aren't paying attention and are too close to the tracks run the risk of being sucked by the air current into the path of the train. That is the reason some of us fall—we have gotten too close!

"And do not lead us into temptation, but deliver us from the evil one." This is a prayer that comes down to us where we rub shoulders with men. It is a prayer that ascends to God from the child of God. There is forgiveness for us today; there is deliverance from temptation and from the evil one. These are three words to look at very closely: *forgiveness, temptation,* and *deliverance*. There is forgiveness with God. The world is hard, cruel, unforgiving, and that spirit has crept into the church, but God can forgive and does forgive on the basis of the blood of Christ. He can make you and me triumphant over our temptations. And He is able to deliver us through the merit, strength, and power of Jesus Christ when you and I take the sword of the Spirit, which is the Word of God, and pray in the Holy Spirit.

FOR YOURS IS THE KINGDOM
AND THE POWER
AND THE GLORY

WE ARE NOW GOING TO LOOK AT SOMETHING that is included in the Lord's Prayer but which probably should be excluded. You see, the words "For Yours is the kingdom and the power and the glory forever" are actually not in the Lord's Prayer.

I would like to give you the Lord's Prayer from the Revised Standard Version, but before doing so I would like to make clear that I do not recommend this version as a substitute for the King James. It is helpful in several places and constitutes a reference book that is useful for any well-grounded Bible student. The prayer is given as follows:

> *Our Father who art in heaven, hallowed be thy name.*
> *Thy kingdom come, thy will be done, on earth as it is in*
> *heaven. Give us this day our daily bread; and forgive us*
> *our debts, as we also have forgiven our debtors; and lead*
> *us not into temptation, but deliver us from evil.*
> (Matthew 6:9–13 RSV)

It stops there and does not go any further. The statement "For Yours is the kingdom and the power and the glory forever," is not included. Now the question naturally arises, why is it that this petition is not included? The reason is that when the King James Version was translated, the translation was made from the best manuscripts in existence at the time. Since then, better manuscripts have been discovered, and we find this petition omitted from these better manuscripts.

Now immediately someone is going to ask, "But how does this fit into the theory of plenary verbal inspiration?" And by "plenary verbal inspiration" we mean that the words of the Bible are inspired. As I see it, that is the only logical explanation of inspiration. Either this is the Word of God or it is not the Word of God. Either it is reliable or it is not reliable. It is not the thoughts that are inspired; it is the words that are inspired. Thoughts can be misunderstood; words cannot.

There is the story of a young lady who had been studying voice, and the time came for her to give her recital. In her dressing room after the concert, she asked about the reaction of her very famous teacher to her performance. A friend, with difficulty, finally brought forth the statement "He said that you sang in a heavenly manner." The young lady, quite thrilled, asked if those were his exact words. The friend said, "Well, those were not his exact words, but that is what he meant." The young singer, still not satisfied, demanded his exact words, which were, "That was an unearthly noise." You see, it is the *words* of Scripture, and not the thoughts, that are important.

We believe in plenary verbal inspiration, but we also believe it applies only to the original documents, most of which have since been lost. But we also believe that the manuscripts we have today are reliable and can be trusted. Many of the manuscripts found have been brought together and all tell the same story. There are some discrepancies, to be sure, but none of these pertain to any of the important doctrines of the Scripture.

Let us look at the matter of inspiration a little further. There is a striking similarity between the written Word and the living Word, who is the Lord Jesus Christ. Both are human and divine. The Lord Jesus Christ is both of God and man. One of the oldest creeds of the church states it accurately: "very man of very man, and very God of very God." Therefore, you would expect to find the "Word of God made flesh" growing weary on a dusty road in Samaria and sitting down to rest. You expect to find Him shedding tears of sorrow at the tomb of Lazarus. Neither is it surprising to hear Him claim to be the Messiah as He talked with the woman of Samaria; nor is it strange to hear Him command Lazarus to come forth from the tomb. He was both God and man.

The Bible is a God-book and it is a man-book. The Word of God has become incarnate in the alphabet of man. The Word of God becomes a book with a binding, printed with printer's ink, and made into words that men can understand.

Men transcribed it by hand even before Gutenberg printed it. It has been translated from one language into another. Scribes have made errors in transcribing the text, and printers have made typographical errors. The limitations imposed upon the Lord Jesus Christ as a man are likewise imposed upon the Bible.

As a human book it requires a knowledge of the language in which it is studied to comprehend its meaning. There is no magic method by which to memorize the fine passages of Scripture. It requires real study as it does to gain a knowledge of any subject—geography, history, literature, or philosophy. The lazy and careless student cannot come at its meaning by any superstitious method. In Proverbs 25:2 (NKJV) we read: "It is the glory of God to conceal a matter, but the glory of kings is to search out a matter." God has hidden rich treasures in His Word, but it requires a great deal of searching to discover them. Diamonds are not on the surface. The injunction is: "Search the Scriptures" (John 5:39 NKJV), "Be diligent to present yourself approved" (2 Timothy 2:15 NKJV), and "Give attention to reading, to exhortation, to doctrine" (1 Timothy 4:13 NKJV).

As a human book, the Bible was written by about forty-five human authors who expressed their thoughts, projected their personalities, and stated their ideas. Nevertheless, they were moved by the Holy Spirit, "for prophecy never came by the will of man, but holy men of God spoke as they were moved by the Holy Spirit" (2 Peter 1:21 NKJV). The Greek word for "move" is *phero*, and it indicates a sailing vessel borne along by the wind. The Spirit of God worked in these men in a way to secure an inerrant Word of God. This is exactly the claim of Scripture:

> **All Scripture is given by inspiration of God, and is profitable for doctrine, for reproof, for correction, for instruction in righteousness.** (2 Timothy 3:16 NKJV)

That word *inspiration* is the Greek *theopneustos*, meaning "God-breathed." Nothing less than the plenary verbal inspiration of Scripture will satisfy the language of Scripture and the need of man.

Although the human authors expressed the full feeling of their hearts and the complete thought of their minds, they nevertheless expressed the exact words of God to men. These men were not pens with which the Spirit of God wrote. Any dictator can make men automatons to express the dictator's thoughts and totally submerge the writer's real intention. The supernatural element in Scripture is that God did not arbitrarily destroy the personality of the writers but instead used them to express His complete, adequate, and inerrant will. The words are God's.

Having completed the canon of Scripture, God has no afterthought to submit as an addendum to the Bible. God perfectly expressed Himself through imperfect men. There is a dual authorship of the Bible that attests to the supernatural. Only God could give a book like the Bible; only

God could send a person like Jesus. We have a God-book. It does not yield merely to human intellect.

The ordinary avenues of knowledge are not sufficient to comprehend its meaning. We get most of our knowledge through the eye gate and the ear gate, but Scripture warns us that these are not adequate to give us divine understanding:

> *But as it is written: "Eye has not seen, nor ear heard, nor have entered into the heart of man the things which God has prepared for those who love Him." But God has revealed them to us through His Spirit. For the Spirit searches all things, yes, the deep things of God.* (1 Corinthians 2:9–10 NKJV)

What the eye gate and ear gate cannot supply, the Spirit of God will compensate. He alone can take divine truths and apply them to our hearts. The facts of Scripture must be learned by human effort, but the spiritual truths must be revealed by the Holy Spirit. The natural man does not have sufficient spiritual IQ to understand the Bible.

> *But the natural man does not receive the things of the Spirit of God, for they are foolishness to him; nor can he know them, because they are spiritually discerned.* (1 Corinthians 2:14 NKJV)

Revelation means that God has communicated with man. Inspiration guarantees the accuracy of that revelation.

Preservation infers that God maintains that revelation in the world.

Illumination insists that only the Holy Spirit has the interpretation for man.

Translation means the transference of the text of Scripture from one language into another.

Now that we have examined the solidarity of the setting in which rests this gem—the Lord's Prayer—let us look again at the phrase that has been omitted in these later translations: "For Yours is the kingdom and the power and the glory forever." It is a most scriptural statement, and for that reason I should like to have it remain as part of the Lord's Prayer. After the people brought their wonderful offerings for the construction of the temple, David lifted his heart to God in prayer:

> *Yours, O LORD, is the greatness, the power and the glory, the victory and the majesty; for all that is in heaven and in earth is Yours; Yours is the kingdom, O LORD, and You are exalted as head over all.* (1 Chronicles 29:11 NKJV)

While David elaborated a great deal, it is a prayer of rare beauty and is basically the same petition that we are considering now.

It is worth noting that in Luke's record we find that the Lord's Prayer, as given there, breaks off at a different point from that given in the Matthew account. I have a notion that the Lord broke off at a different place on each occasion of repeating the prayer. And the reason is obvious, for I feel He was attempting to teach something. Since the prayer as recorded in Luke 11:2–4 carried no "amen," it was thus open to added petitions. It was given to babes in Christ that they might know how to pray. It is the same as how we today teach our little folk to say, "Now I lay me down to sleep . . ." Before long they have added, "And bless Mommy and Daddy," and later, other petitions.

I must confess that several times I have had to get up off my knees and tiptoe out of the room because of some of the things for which my little girl has prayed. I know that the Lord understood her prayers, but I have never discovered why she prays for the little boys and girls in China and then for the boys and girls in Michigan. I do not know why Michigan should be chosen out of the fifty states. These little ones just launch out into the deep, and in this lies our illustration of the absence of the "amen."

YOURS IS THE KINGDOM . . .

Now, let us look at the three possessions of our God mentioned here. First is the kingdom. We have a great deal to say about the kingdom, and I make no apologies in going over some of this again, for repetition is a sound principle of pedagogy.

Let us remember that in the magnificent Old Testament prayer, David had in mind the kingdom God had promised to him—that from his line there would come the Anointed One, the Messiah, the Christ, and He would sit upon the throne of David and rule on this earth. As David lifted his heart to God in prayer, he saw a kingdom lying in the future; he saw that kingdom as a mighty focal point with the great rays of Scripture converging upon it. That is my reason for saying that the church is in the kingdom and we are moving toward that day when the kingdom shall be established.

The Father said to the Son, "Sit at My right hand, till I make Your enemies Your footstool" (Psalm 110:1 NKJV). After His rejection, Christ was brought to death through crucifixion, was buried, rose from the dead, ascended back to heaven, and took His place at God's right hand. And today He is bringing many sons home to glory. Thus He is moving world events toward the focal point when this kingdom shall be established upon the earth, He shall reign from shore to shore, righteousness shall cover this earth as the waters cover the sea, and righteousness and peace shall kiss each other.

We must remember that this kingdom will not come by human manipulation. It will not come by ecumenical movements or any man-made program. It will be established in one way, and that is by the catastrophic and cataclysmic coming of Christ to this earth to put down all unrighteousness and establish His kingdom here in power and glory. And that is what you express when you say, "Yours is the kingdom."

. . . AND THE POWER . . .

But, my beloved, let us move on to the second possession: "the power." This is an age of power. It is an age of jet planes, rockets for outer space, and nuclear warheads. But in this age of power, when unheard-of things are being accomplished in a material world, it has become the age of powerlessness for the church. As Samson was shorn of his hair, thus has the church been robbed of her power.

I'm reminded of Thomas Aquinas who entered the place where the pope was counting the money. Thinking he had entered at a time when he should not have, he turned to walk away. But the pope saw him and said, "Sir Thomas, no longer can the church say, 'Silver and gold have I none.'" Without even turning to look back, Thomas Aquinas said, "That is right, Your Holiness, but no longer can the church say to the impotent man, 'Rise and walk.'"

This is an age of powerlessness, and yet:

[He is] *declared to be the Son of God with power according to the Spirit of holiness, by the resurrection from the dead.* (Romans 1:4 NKJV)

He also said,

All authority [power] *has been given to Me in heaven and on earth.* (Matthew 28:18 NKJV)

And further:

> **But you shall receive power when the Holy Spirit has come upon you.** (Acts 1:8 NKJV)

How can these things be? Let us look at the common logic of it. If the electric lights go out in Los Angeles, it does not mean that Hoover Dam has given way. It simply means that somewhere a connection has been broken. Now Christ has had all power given to Him, and if your church is powerless, then some of you had better be walking the line to see where the connection has been broken. Do you recall the incident of the man at the foot of the Mount of Transfiguration? He had the little lad who was demon pos-sessed, and he said, "So I brought him to Your disciples, but they could not cure him" (Matthew 17:16 NKJV). How true that is of us today. It should cause us to bow our heads in prayer. Perhaps He cannot trust us with power today because we abuse or misuse it. But thank God He is coming and He will use power to correct the evils of this world. It will take power to get rid of our political regimes. It will take power to put Christ on the Throne. He is coming in power! His is the kingdom, the power!

. . . AND THE GLORY

And now let us come to "the glory." What is glory? What is its shape, size, and color? Perhaps you feel that you have never seen it, or you believe that it is spiritual and therefore cannot be seen. Not so, my friend. It can be seen. Every Hebrew word translated as our English word *glory* means something physical. It has been a rich experience for me to go through these words in order to arrive at their real meaning. How my heart longs to see the glory! I trust that you will be interested to look at these words also.

The first "glory" means "wide and great" as in this verse: "The heavens declare the glory of God" (Psalm 19:1 NKJV). I never look into the starry heavens but that I am reminded of the greatness and vastness of His glory. Oh, the vastness of the universe! And did you know that it is expanding continually? Surely "the heavens declare the glory of God."

Then there is another word associated with our word *glory,* and it means "brightness." And there is a third word that is translated "beauty," as in "Even Solomon in all his glory was not arrayed like one of these" (Matthew 6:29 NKJV), referring to the lilies of the field. Just as this universe reveals the vastness of God, so a little flower reveals something of the beauty of God. The One who made the flowers loves beauty, and God is the One who made the flowers.

But the most common word in the Old Testament relative to the glory of God is the Hebrew word *kabod,* which means "wealth and worth; dignity and honor; splendor and majesty" and can apply either to God or man. Its primary meaning is that of the external or physical, but it also has an ethical and moral significance. When used, it speaks of the purity and holiness of God; it speaks of His essential character:

> *I am the LORD, that is My name; and My glory I will not give to another, nor My praise to carved images.* (Isaiah 42:8 NKJV)

Now this word *glory* as used in the Old Testament speaks of a material manifestation of God. God said to Moses on Mount Sinai, "You cannot see My face, but I'll let you see My glory" (see Exodus 33:20–23). Moses saw God's glory on another occasion, too. We read that when the tabernacle was completed, the glory of the Lord filled the place. And when Moses and Aaron moved out with the Israelites, the shekinah presence of God was with them in the form of a pillar of cloud by day and fire by night. It was a physical manifestation of God. You may recall that when Solomon built the temple, the glory was transferred from the tabernacle to the temple. But somewhere in the Israelites' long, dreary, sinful history, the glory departed. Ezekiel saw the vision—it lifted up from the temple, went on out to the Mount of Olives, and was caught back into heaven. That was the last view of the shekinah glory. (See Ezekiel 8–10.)

Then after four hundred years of silence, shepherds on a hillside had a manifestation of the glory of God as the angel said, "Glory to God in the highest." As John said:

> **And the Word became flesh and dwelt among us** [pitched
> His tent among us]**, and we beheld His glory, the glory as
> of the only begotten of the Father, full of grace and truth.**
> (John 1:14 NKJV)

May I say that the word *glory* has an ethical value here,
because in Christ it was not physically manifested except
on one or two occasions. What they saw was that He was
innately holy, harmless, undefiled, the One separate from
sinners. But when He was born, He laid aside His glory that
He had with the Father in heaven. The thing that had
identified God in the Old Testament no longer identified
Him. In the New Testament, we find Him wrapped in the
swaddling clothes of humanity and, in due time, grown to
full manhood and the service of the ministry. He laid aside
that physical manifestation as a garment. In writing of it
Paul said:

> **. . . Who, being in the form of God** [the *morphia* of God]**,
> did not consider it robbery to be equal with God** [because
> it rightfully belonged to Him]**, but** [laid it aside and] **made
> Himself of no reputation, taking the form of a bondser-
> vant, and coming in the likeness of men.** (Philippians
> 2:6–7 NKJV)

For more than two thousand years, theologians have
been arguing about what it was that He laid aside. What was
it that He emptied Himself of? I feel that He laid aside His

glory and walked this earth as a man. Oh, He is God, but He laid aside His glory. Then there came that day when He walked with His disciples and "a cloud received Him out of their sight" (Acts 1:9 NKJV). It was not a rain cloud. It was the glory-cloud—the shekinah glory. That which He had laid aside was waiting for Him, and thus He took, again, all the prerogatives that rightfully were His. He wore it as a garment and entered into heaven!

At this point of departure He made a statement that we will do well to meditate upon. In telling His disciples that He was coming again, He said,

> *Then the sign of the Son of Man will appear in heaven, and then all the tribes of the earth will mourn, and they will see the Son of Man coming on the clouds of heaven with power and great glory.* (Matthew 24:30 NKJV)

Have you ever stopped to think what that sign is going to be? I am not sure that I know, but I would like to make a suggestion. Personally, I feel that when He is to come, the shekinah glory will flash as the lightning from the east to the west. Thus shekinah glory will again be revealed upon the earth. There is no glory today—it is withheld. Today you and I are to glorify Him. He said:

> *Let your light so shine before men, that they may see your good works and glorify your Father in heaven.* (Matthew 5:16 NKJV)

And Paul said:

> *Therefore, whether you eat or drink, or whatever you do,*
> *do all to the glory of God.* (1 Corinthians 10:31 NKJV)

That is the chief business of a Christian. Some will say that soul-winning is the Christian's chief end. No, that is secondary. To glorify God is our primary business as a professing Christian. Scripture has a word for us here:

> *Now thanks be to God who always leads us in triumph in*
> *Christ, and through us diffuses the fragrance of His*
> *knowledge in every place. For we are to God the fragrance*
> *of Christ among those who are being saved and among*
> *those who are perishing.* (2 Corinthians 2:14–15 NKJV)

You and I are to glorify God regardless of results. We are to glorify Him and bring nothing of disrepute on His name or cause that will drive men and women from His presence. Someday that is what we will spend an eternity doing—glorifying Him. If you do not enjoy glorifying Him here, then I do not think you will enjoy heaven very much. In all fairness, how can you—after thinking quietly upon the undeserved love and goodness of God poured out upon you—fail to want to kneel before Him thankfully in adoration?

"For Yours is the kingdom and the power and the glory forever."

Chapter 18

THE GRAND OMISSION

WHEN YOU SEE A FREIGHT TRAIN STANDING on the track with a caboose coupled on, you know that it is ready to take to the road—it is complete. A freight train with other cars added after the caboose would look irregular. And should you see a freight train without a caboose, the instant impression would be that something else is to be added. With this simple illustration before us, let us consider the matter of the Lord Jesus breaking off the Lord's Prayer at different points and under different conditions without using the word *amen*.

Now, the fact that He omitted the *amen* in the instance recorded in Luke 11 meant that something else was to be added. But what right have we to add anything to the Lord's Prayer? I would like to say, hastily, that we can add only Scripture to the Lord's Prayer, and we must have scriptural warrant for it. The question is, do we have scriptural warrant to do this? And if so, what is it that we are to add? What is the grand omission that creates this great void?

Now, the Lord Jesus gave the Lord's Prayer to His disciples at the beginning of His ministry, and He repeated it intermittently. He must have said it many, many times. Then at the end of His ministry, He met with His disciples in the Upper Room, where He instituted the Lord's Supper. Then He told them something new: He told them that He was the Vine and they were the branches. And then He gave them a new basis for prayer. What He said was very vital, but it is passed over today:

> **And in that day** [when He comes back from the dead, after His death and resurrection] **you will ask Me nothing** [that is, we are not to pray to Him]. **Most assuredly, I say to you, whatever you ask the Father in My name He will give you. Until now you have asked nothing in My name. Ask, and you will receive, that your joy may be full.** (John 16:23–24 NKJV)

And here is our scriptural warrant: we are told to add to the Lord's Prayer "in the name of Christ." This is a new basis of prayer.

Back in the Old Testament, prayer was made for the glory of God based on the covenants of God. That is the reason you find so many times in the Old Testament that when men prayed to God they spoke of "the God of Abraham, the God of Isaac, and the God of Jacob"—the covenant-making and covenant-keeping God. When we come to the New Testament and the Lord's Prayer, we find that it is made for the glory of God. But something new has been added. The Lord Jesus says in effect: "Up to this point you have asked nothing in My name, but from now on ask in My name." And, beloved, the Lord's Prayer, as well as any prayer today, should be made in the name of Christ. In fact, there is a startling promise given here:

> **And whatever you ask in My name, that I will do, that the Father may be glorified in the Son. If you ask anything in My name, I will do it.** (John 14:13–14 NKJV)

He not only said it once, He said it three times in the Upper Room (see John 15:16). I say to you that this is a startling promise! It is startling because it is limitless, it is without bounds: "If you ask anything in My name . . ."

But it is qualified, and it is qualified by "in My name"—that is, the name of Christ. In this day in which we are living, it is the only basis for prayer—the neglected act of worship. And we are to remember that God hears only the prayer that is made in the name of Christ; there is no other basis. But that He has promised to hear prayer made on this basis, we may rest assured.

Here it is important to understand what it means to pray in the name of Christ. It is not a formula, a prescription, or a pet expression with which to conclude prayer. Nor is it a turning on of the spigot, or the writing of a letter to Santa Claus. Oh, no, it is not that at all. So what is the real meaning?

To pray in the name of Christ means, first of all, that the individual praying must himself be in Christ. There is a word that, over time, has come to mean more to me than any other word. It seems to increase in richness and value day by day. It is a little preposition, and you will probably be surprised to hear it. The most important word in the Bible to me is *in*—*in* Christ. "In Christ" is another way of speaking of salvation. Dr. Norman B. Harrison said that identification is synonymous with salvation. How true that is! The most profound statement that I find in the Word of God is "You in Me, and I in You" (John 14:20 NKJV). Those are simple words—any six-year-old can tell you the meaning of each word—but, beloved, how profound they are when put together in this statement!

What does it mean that He is "in" us? Well, He took our place down here.

> *For He made Him who knew no sin to be sin for us, that we might become the righteousness of God in Him.* (2 Corinthians 5:21 NKJV)

He was made sin for us—not in some academic manner, some forensic way, but He actually was made sin for us. And the moment that holy Lamb of God—who was in perfect fellowship with the Father, for He said, "And yet I am not alone, because the Father is with Me" (John 16:32 NKJV)—

bore our sins upon the cross, He was completely identified with us. He was "delivered up because of our offenses, and was raised because of our justification" (Romans 4:25 NKJV). Today we are told that in Christ we have forgiveness of sins. Today God is saving men because Christ completely identified Himself with us, paying the penalty in full for your sin and mine.

Now I would like to say very reverently that God is no chiseler—He is not a shady character or a swindler. He has collected for your sin; the penalty was paid by Christ. God will save a sinner 100 percent because Christ was identified in us down here. But that is just one half of the story.

We are now identified in Him. He was "raised because of our justification," but justification is not forgiveness of sin. So He was made sin for us "that we might become the righteousness of God in Him." He paid the penalty of sin completely. Jesus has "paid it all, all to Him I owe." That is my favorite hymn, and at my funeral I do not want them to sing "Safe in the Arms of Jesus" or "Beautiful Isle of Somewhere." I want them to sing the positive hymn of salvation in which we can live gloriously and die triumphantly—"Jesus paid it all . . . Sin had left a crimson stain, He washed it white as snow."[1] He paid it all, and now His robe of righteousness has been made over and given to those who do no more nor less than simply trust in the Lord Jesus Christ.

There was a book published years ago that told a fictional tale of the robe that was worn by Christ at the time of His crucifixion. Actually, that robe had no romantic history. Probably some burly Roman soldier won the robe, it fit him too well, and with summer coming on in a very hot climate, he could not bear its heat and threw it into a corner. One day someone picked it up and threw it away. You say, "Oh, my, that is awful!" No, my friend, that robe has no romantic history because there was no merit in it at all. God saw to it that it disappeared.

But thank God that there is another robe—the robe of His righteousness. And that robe does have a romantic history. Oh, how romantic it is! That robe is spotless and white, and He puts it over any and every sinner who will only trust Christ. No longer do we have our sins upon us, for Christ bore them. Now we are more than forgiven sinners; we stand in robes of righteousness in God's presence, complete in Christ. Nothing is to be added, for nothing can make us more complete than we are in Jesus Christ—saved and brought into His presence, accepted on the basis of what He has done.

You may remember that Jacob, by his mother's trickery, got hold of Esau's garment, put it on, and deceived his blind father who thought Jacob was Esau partly because he was clothed in Esau's garment. When I come into God's presence, He accepts me as Christ not because I am deceiving Him, not because He cannot see me, but because it is the way God has arranged it. I am clothed in Christ's robe of righteousness. I am accepted "in" Him, and now I can come in Christ and present my petitions to God. It means that when I pray in the name of Christ, I can do so because I am in Christ. We must be children of God before we are ever on praying ground, "for the eyes of the LORD are on the righteous, and His ears are open to their prayers; but the face of the LORD is against those who do evil" (1 Peter 3:12 NKJV).

The child of God should be admonished by the glorious things said in Hebrews:

> *Seeing then that we have a great High Priest who has passed through the heavens, Jesus the Son of God, let us hold fast our confession . . . Let us therefore come boldly to the throne of grace, that we may obtain mercy and find grace to help in time of need.* (Hebrews 4:14, 16 NKJV)

To pray in the name of Christ means that we can come boldly because He has signed His name with ours in the petition that we make. In my first year of college, I did not have enough money to get through and wanted to borrow some. But I will be honest with you and say that I could not find anyone who wanted to lend me any. Finally, a wonderful friend of mine said he would cosign a note with me. He put his name on that note, I took it to the bank, and I had no difficulty at all. They did not even look at my name, but they saw his name, accepted it, and let me have the money.

Now, in simple language, God will not hear your prayers because of who you are, and He will not hear your prayers because of your merit. He hears your prayers and my prayers only when they are made in the name of Christ. If Christ's name is on the petition, God hears and answers.

There is a second thing that is important as well: when we pray in the name of Christ, the prayer must be in the will of God. That is, the person as well as the prayer must be in the will of God. Notice this carefully:

If you love Me, keep My commandments. (John 14:15 NKJV)

Keeping His commandments is to be in the will of God. He says:

If you abide in Me, and My words abide in you, you will ask what you desire, and it shall be done for you. (John 15:7 NKJV)

It is not only union with Christ, but it is communion with Him that gives a basis for God hearing and answering prayer.

Prayer is not a matter of attempting to get a reluctant Deity to come over on our side; prayer is not a method resorted to as if to persuade God to do something that He is loath to do. Think carefully! God is trying to persuade us! He wants to do something for us, and He is trying to get us into a position to receive it. Recall the Lord Jesus' parable by contrast that is recorded in Luke 18. A poor widow went every day to that judge, and finally he heard her petition. The Lord Jesus says that if that unjust judge would hear a poor widow who had no political influence, don't you know your Father in heaven, who is not unjust, will hear you? God is trying to get us into a place where He can bless us!

Our earnest prayer, as children of God, should be: "Lord, get us into a position where we can be blessed. Take out of our hearts those things that are blocking You from getting through in mighty power." God *wants* to bless—need we try to persuade Him to do something that He longs to do?

Your prayers and mine are not going to upset the program of God, for it is in God's program that prayer shall have a place. It is interesting that God has never sent a blessing to His people without first having them pray for that blessing. I know that in my own experience God has had me praying for things that were already on the way, and He does that many times today. Daniel prayed that the people might go out of captivity even though he already had God's word that they were to leave at the end of seventy years. Daniel prayed because it was God's will. There are many ways of escape in the minds of people today, but God has only one method and that is prayer.

I want to conclude with a very homely illustration. Suppose there is a man who wants to master the violin. So he finds a station on his radio that is playing the music of Bach. He sits in front of the speaker and attempts to play along on his violin, but he is not experienced enough and is not able to keep up. He makes mistake after mistake and, growing weary of his efforts, begins to play "Turkey in the

Straw"—a tune he knows well—instead. This in no way affects the artistry of the music being played over the radio.

The next evening, the man tunes in again and this time they are broadcasting a piece by Wagner. Once again, he attempts to follow along on his violin. But once more it ends in failure, and he resorts to the cowboy music with which he is familiar. Again, this does not at all interrupt the perfection and beauty of the concert over the radio.

But this man, longing to play, hears that Handel's *Messiah* is going to be given the following week. So he spends the days and evenings practicing the score. And when at last the strains of the *Messiah* come from the radio, the man is ready to join in under the director and go along in harmony.

Beloved, that is what it means to pray in the name of Christ. It means for you and me to get in tune with heaven. It does not mean that God must rearrange His program for us, but that He will work mightily upon us if we get our little instrument in tune so that whatsoever we ask, He will do.

Regardless of the prayer you pray, whether it be the Lord's Prayer or another, there is a grand omission unless it is made in the name of Christ. And it cannot be made in the name of Christ until you are *in* Christ, fully trusting Him, and you are in the will of God.

NOTES

CHAPTER 1
1. James Montgomery, "At Home in Heaven."
2. *Hamlet*, act 3, scene 1, line 55.

CHAPTER 2
1. Author unknown.

CHAPTER 3
1. Howard, P.E., Jr., "Glimpses of Earlier Revivals," in *How Prayer Brings Revival* (Philadelphia: Appleman Evangelistic Campaign, n.d.), 4–6.

CHAPTER 5
1. Elisha Hoffman, "I Must Tell Jesus," public domain.

CHAPTER 8
1. Author unknown.

CHAPTER 14

1. Author unknown.
2. "Pippa Passes," part I, lines 221–228.
3. *Hamlet*, act 1, scene 4, line 90.

CHAPTER 15

1. Author unknown.
2. Author unknown.
3. Author unknown.

CHAPTER 18

1. Elvina M. Hall, "Jesus Paid It All," public domain.